THE INVISIBLE VETERAN

Kevin Kidder

Ballast Books, LLC
www.ballastbooks.com

ISBN: 978-1-966786-94-8 (Paperback)
ISBN: 978-1-966786-95-5 (E-book)

Printed in Hong Kong

Published by Ballast Books
www.ballastbooks.com

For more information, bulk orders, appearances,
or speaking requests,
please email: info@ballastbooks.com

DEDICATION

To the men and women who wore the uniform, and to the ones who stood beside them.

To every veteran who has ever wondered whether their story still matters: This book is for you.

To my children: May you always know that your dad's greatest mission is to love you, guide you, and cheer you on in every chapter of your own journey.

To my stepfather, Robert Lee Vaughan, an army medic during the Cold War and the truest example of what it means to be an invisible veteran. He rarely sought recognition and was often reluctant to even call himself a veteran, yet his service mattered deeply. He was the reason I joined the army, a staunch supporter throughout my military career, and a man of quiet intelligence, patience, and unwavering faith. He loved my mother faithfully and lived with humility and integrity. He passed away on January 12, 2024, but his influence lives on in me, in this book, and in every life he touched.

And above all, to the One who gave me the strength to keep going: This book is an offering of gratitude. May every page reflect the truth that real purpose, identity, and connection are found in Christ, whose love never leaves us invisible.

PROLOGUE

"Our deepest fear is not that we are inadequate.
Our deepest fear is that we are powerful beyond measure.
It is our light, not our darkness, that most frightens us.
We ask ourselves, *Who am I to be brilliant, gorgeous, talented, fabulous?*
Actually, who are you not to be? You are a child of God.
Your playing small does not serve the world.
There is nothing enlightened about shrinking
so that other people won't feel insecure around you.
We are all meant to shine, as children do.
We were born to make manifest
the glory of God that is within us.
It's not just in some of us; it's in everyone.
And as we let our own light shine, we unconsciously give other people permission to do the same.
As we are liberated from our own fear,
our presence automatically liberates others."

—*Marianne Williamson*

INTRODUCTION

THE BOTTOM LINE UP FRONT (BLUF)

I am not your typical veteran author. I wasn't an "operator." I don't have movie-worthy stories. I'm just a regular army guy who thoroughly enjoyed serving his country for twenty years.

This book is for the veteran who feels unseen. For the one who gave everything in uniform and then walked into a world that didn't know what to do with them. It's for the man or woman who looks in the mirror and asks, "What now?"

The truth is that transition is brutal. Not because you're weak but because you've been forged in a world with a different language, a different pace, a different standard.

And when that world ends, it doesn't just feel like changing career paths. It feels like a loss of self.

I know because I've lived it.

Deployments. Combat. Leadership. Awards. Loss. I know what it's like to be responsible for lives. And I know what it's like to come home, hang up the uniform, and feel invisible.

But I also know this: You are not alone. And you are not done. Not even close.

Throughout this book, I'll share parts of my journey, not to impress you but to walk beside you. To show you that the pain you're feeling isn't weakness; it's a signal. And it's time to respond.

I'm not a therapist. I'm not a guru. I'm a husband. A father. A coach. A man of faith. A warrior still trying to lead in any way I can.

If you're a veteran, a family member of one, or someone trying to understand . . . this book is for you.

So let's get to it. Let's stop surviving and start thriving. Let's stop hiding and start healing. Let's stop waiting for the eulogy and start living the legacy.

Because the world is better with you in it. And it's time for you to believe that again.

CHAPTER 1

THE MOMENT NO ONE PREPARES YOU FOR

You didn't just leave a job. You left a way of life.

My Story: From Soldier to Civilian

As much as I loved my time in the army, I was ready for retirement. I only wanted to do twenty years because that fall was when my son would turn fourteen and start high school.

My son, Ty, was your typical preteen and teenager, except he has always had the kindest heart and has always been the sweetest boy. Something notable about him is that he always despised being dirty. He would go outside and play, traipsing all over the base and housing areas where we lived, but once he was done, he wanted to be clean. He couldn't stand his hands being dirty at all. It was easy enough for him to stay neat and clean when he was playing video games, something he loved to do, but he had to get his hands dirty when playing sports. Ty didn't shy away from the sweat and grime of hard work when he played baseball, football, and basketball. But you can bet he cleaned up quick when the game was over! I was proud to cheer him on during his games and even help with scorekeeping and coaching (more on this later).

Ty also loved to go fishing. In fact, he caught his first fish (a bluegill) in one of our kayaks on the lake when we lived in the lake community in North Carolina. It's a cherished memory I have with my son—just one of many.

My daughter, Juliana, loved to dress up like a princess and embrace her girly nature, but she also played sports—basketball and then competitive cheer. She loved to bake and go with me to the grocery store (especially during the COVID-19 pandemic) to buy new desserts from the bakery. I remember we were on a lemon kick the summer of my transition.

Juliana was my snuggle bug. We watched *Forged in Fire* together religiously. Something special about her is that she has the best, most contagious laugh. When we put on YouTube and watch epic fails, the house (and neighborhood, if the window is open) echoes with her distinct laugh. Once she gets going, she can't stop, and it's a futile effort to suppress your own laughter. Her laughing fits are so infectious that my mom and son have both contracted the disease in public—to the point that people stopped, stared, and made comments about it! I don't care—I think it's hysterical. Juliana has always known who she is and what she likes and what she doesn't. She is very comfortable in her own skin and really doesn't care what other people think. Other than perhaps her big brother, whom she has ADORED her whole life.

To put it simply, my kids have always been my world. From personal and professional experience, I know the value and importance a father brings by being present during those formative teenage years. So I dropped my retirement packet in January 2020, exactly one year before I would have hit twenty years in the army. We were deployed to Poland at the time. I had just finished my bachelor's degree the month prior, and I had pretty much bombarded my S-1 (the army equivalent of human resources) with my presence multiple times a day, ensuring my packet was good to go. Because we were forward deployed, it took a little more effort and time for things to get approved back home at Fort Bragg, but all in all, it was a smooth process, and my packet was approved before we returned home stateside.

A few days before we were supposed to fly home from Poland, some weird virus was causing a ruckus *everywhere*. Perhaps you're familiar with it. I'm talking about COVID-19, of course! There was a real concern we would not go home on time and our deployment would be extended. I was nervous. I wanted to be home. I was ready to start the next chapter of my life and was ready for the opportunity to prepare for it. I had given nineteen years to my country and was looking forward to what life after the military would be like. Luckily, the extension did not happen, and we were back home as scheduled in mid-February. We went on block leave, and I was able to knock out all of my Army Career and Alumni Program (ACAP) appointments before the shutdown hit.

The thing about working for the government is that when new policies are put in place, you follow them immediately. For me, the timing couldn't have been better. I only had a few follow-up ACAP appointments, which could be done virtually, and due to phenomenal leadership, I didn't really have a job; I was told to focus on my future. When the "essential personnel only" order came out, I knew that didn't apply to me, which resulted in me having a dream retirement process. I'd get up in the morning, go for a run or a ruck, come home, drink coffee, eat breakfast, and read for a little bit. If I needed to, I would run to the office to knock out paperwork, but I was rarely there for more than an hour or two.

At this point in time, we lived in a wonderful lake community, and it was only two miles from my front door to the lake. So, when I'd get done at the office, and if the weather was nice, I'd back my truck up the slight incline of the driveway and set the parking brake. Then I'd walk back to the boat, remove the chock, and lower the coupler onto the hitch of my truck before grabbing my kids and heading to the lake. The kids and I would do physical training (PT) at the beach of the lake, normally a modified SEAL workout with push-ups, pull-ups, sprints, etc., where we would get wet 'n' sandy. Or we'd do a mini "triathlon," where we'd add some swimming at the end of our on-land exercises. After that, we'd launch the boat, find the part of the lake we wanted, jump off the back, and swim or go tubing. We'd be out there all day before finally going home and finding something fun to eat.

You know that feeling: You've got that post-lake sunburn because you forgot to reapply sunscreen. It doesn't hurt except when you smile. You're famished because you depleted all your fuel splashing around in the water, and you're pleasantly exhausted from playing all day. Water runs down your chin as you chug it from a plastic cup like a nomad lost in the Sahara.

That was my life most days, and it was incredible. We'd come home and make a sandwich, which always got stuck to the roofs of our mouths because no matter how much water we chugged, we were still a little dehydrated. After scarfing down some chips, we'd get that late afternoon post-lake nap. Not a planned nap but rather that sinking-into-the-couch, feeling-the-stress-melt-away, suddenly-your-eyes-are-heavy-after-being-in-the-sun-all-day kinda nap.

North Carolina weather is awesome, although the humidity can be daunting. In the evening, it cools down, so I'd get the smoker going. Soft winds would traverse through the trees, and a present but not overwhelming scent of pine would hang in the air.

First, I'd grab my charcoal chimney and set it on the grates of the grill before adding the charcoal, setting it on fire, and getting it white-hot. I loved watching the mini towering inferno dissipate into a smoldering fire.

From there, I'd remove the grates and pour the coals into the bottom of my offset stick burner. I'd get a mini fireworks display as the coals hit the bottom and each other. Then, I'd put the grates back on and check the cooking zones with my hand to ensure the surface was ready.

Next came the best part: the sizzle of marinated meat brought up to room temperature being gently placed onto hot metal. We are a far cry from our neanderthal ancestors, but there's still something primal about putting meat over a fire to cook it. When I grill and BBQ, I go low and slow. I would build and develop flavors that slowly but steadily replaced the scent of pine in the air. I cooked around 275 degrees to layer and build flavor—oak, mesquite, salt, pepper, garlic, onion, and rendering fat. This process also allowed me time to indulge in a cold beverage.

Once the meat was where I needed it to be, I'd throw on some veggies—asparagus or squash and zucchini brushed with olive oil and seasoning—and place them in the hotter cooking zone so they could be kissed by the fire and develop a nice char without getting overcooked.

After dinner, we'd watch TV, a movie, or YouTube, which always resulted in a laughing fit from my daughter. That would spread like wildfire because she has an infectious laugh. Then it was time for bed, and as I lay my head down, I hoped for another day just like today.

As delightful as those days were, once it officially hit, retirement wasn't all fun in the sun. I was facing a "duality of man" type of complex the day I retired. Professionally, I was ready to embark on a new-ish career. To be honest, I was tired of the politics and bureaucracy and seeing people get promoted over me. A lot of this was my own fault, but the frustration remained. I was also excited for the potential freedom that came with a fresh start. I envisioned myself having a distinguished law enforcement career culminating with a Jesse Stone–type arc, where I'd retire as the police chief of a small, tight-knit lake community somewhere.

But personally, I was terrified. As I'll describe in more detail shortly, my marriage was in a very precarious spot, and I knew that the end was potentially looming. I was cognizant of the suicide rate of veterans, especially recently divorced veterans, and was concerned I might not be strong enough to handle the devastation. I was becoming too comfortable with the idea of being Clint Eastwood's character in *Gran Torino*, just growing old, cranky, crotchety, mad at the world, and isolated from everyone.

The light of hope for the next chapter of my professional life was largely obliterated by the fear and distress overwhelming my heart. My sense of self was thrown off kilter, and as I'd come to find out, I had a lot of work to do on myself to recalibrate and find purpose again.

The Day After the Uniform

My last day in uniform was September 30, 2020, and I started terminal leave on October 3, 2020, before officially retiring on February 1, 2021. Each of these occasions was momentous, unforgettable. But it was taking off my uniform for the last time that instigated a monumental shift. It didn't feel like retirement; it felt like being dropped into a vacuum.

There's no ceremony for the first day out. No formation. No final radio check. No one handing you a new mission or reminding you to hydrate. Just quiet.

After twenty years in uniform, I had those four months of terminal leave. No briefings. No structure. No soldiers to check on. I didn't have to be anywhere. There was nowhere to report.

And in the stillness of that first morning, I sat on the edge of my bed and felt something I hadn't felt in years—completely untethered. It should've felt like freedom. But it didn't. It felt like loss.

While the world was in lockdown, I was unraveling in my own kind of isolation. No more team. No more mission. No more role. Just a man in his late thirties trying to figure out who he was without the rank, the patch, or the uniform.

And that's when the invisibility started. It doesn't happen like flicking a light switch; it creeps in. You begin to notice that people don't ask about your service anymore.

They assume you're "good" now. You've got your DD-214. Maybe a retirement check. Maybe a few medals.

From the outside, you've made it. But inside? You feel like a ghost in your own life.

Because no one tells you this part: The uniform comes off in a day. But the identity—that takes years to rebuild. If you even try at all.

Some vets push it down. Some numb it out. Some pretend they never miss it. Some never make it through.

But here's why I wrote this book: Because I believe you can make it through. Not just to survive but to thrive. To lead again. To realize you *matter* again.

This chapter—the first one—is about calling it what it is. This is the moment no one talks about. The moment you're home but not whole, free but floating.

If that's you, let me tell you something right now: You are not broken. You are rebuilding. And this silence? It's not your end.

It's your new beginning.

What That Day Really Looked Like

When I talk about that specific day, it's easy to let it sound neat, clean, and cinematic. It wasn't.

The lease on the house my family had lived in, part of that quiet lake community I previously described, had expired. My wife and kids had already moved back to Michigan a few months before (more on this later).

I stayed behind to finish my out-processing and all the other retirement requirements.

On that morning, I wasn't waking up in a home. I was waking up in a buddy's guest room, thankful for a roof but feeling more displaced than ever. I had a twelve-hour drive ahead of me, heading north toward a life I knew was fracturing before my eyes.

Leadership—the thing I loved, the thing I thrived on—was gone. The pride of serving, of sacrificing, of being a part of something bigger than myself had been reduced to a few framed certificates and a pile of gear packed into the bed of my truck.

And the thing no one really prepares you for—the thing the army's transition program completely misses—is the *structure* you lose.

In the military, everything has structure. Right place, right time, right uniform. Follow the commander's intent. Stay within the lines.

Now? Now there were no lines. There was no map. There was no code of conduct anyone else followed. It was chaos. And it felt like stepping into a gunfight naked, exposed, unarmed.

Was I proud to retire? Absolutely.

But pride and shame don't cancel each other out. They coexist. Part of me was proud. Part of me was embarrassed—because as much as I loved my career, I'd left at the lowest retirement-eligible rank.

In the army, that carries a stigma. It whispers in the back of your mind: You could have done more. You could have *been* more.

And that whisper grows louder in the silence if you let it.

But what I didn't understand back then—and what I hope you start to see—is that the military didn't make me valuable. It magnified what was already there.

My mission didn't end. It just changed.

Reflection and Recon

- Where were you the day your uniform came off?
- What part of your identity felt strongest while you served?
- What part felt most vulnerable after you left?
- Were you prepared for the transition, or did it feel like being dropped into chaos?
- How did you expect to feel versus how did you actually feel?
- Have you allowed yourself to grieve the transition?
- What has the silence taught you about yourself so far?
- Do you believe you still have a mission?
- If you could speak to the version of yourself from that first day, what would you say?

Call to Action: Own Your First Day

I was fortunate to attend the US Army's Joint Personnel Recovery Course, a program designed to prepare service members for the unthinkable: capture, isolation, and the long road to coming home. One of the most powerful lessons I took away had nothing to do with evasion tactics or rescue procedures. It was about what happens after.

When someone survives an ordeal—combat, captivity, a near-death experience—it can take a long time for the mind to find steady ground again. Instructors told us recovery isn't just about physical safety. It's about *owning your story*. The people who heal best are the ones who learn to tell their story again and again until it stops owning them.

At first, the story pours out in vivid detail. You replay every moment, every sound, every smell. But as you tell it more, something shifts. The version gets shorter. The edges soften. The rawness fades. And somewhere in that process, you reclaim a piece of yourself.

And that's what I want for you.

Before you move to the next section, write down the story of your first day out. If you can't or don't want to write it out, then say it out loud—while walking around your house, in the shower, on a walk in the park, or next to the beach, lake, river . . . just get it out there.

Where were you? What did you feel? What did you hope for, and what did you fear?

Be brutally honest. Not for the world. For you. Because naming the day you left the uniform behind is the first step to building the life you're meant to lead.

Your first day—whatever it looked like—wasn't just about surviving it. It was your flag in the ground, the moment you claimed your next chapter. Don't wait for the perfect time. Write it. Speak it. Tell it to the mirror if you have to. Because every time you do, you're proving the story belongs to you. *Not the other way around.*

The Identity Void

The day I joined the army, I became part of something bigger than myself. The day I left it, I didn't realize how much of me I had handed over to the mission. For twenty years, I had a uniform that told people who I was before I said a word. It came with rank. With respect. With clarity.

Every day, I had a role. I had a chain of command. I had a sense of purpose, even when the job was tough. *Especially* when it was tough.

Then suddenly . . . it was gone. No more title. No more formation. No more "Sergeant Kidder."

That kind of identity doesn't just go away; you have to peel it off. Layer by layer. And underneath? For a lot of us, there's confusion. There's grief. There's guilt.

Who am I now? That's the question we avoid but can't outrun.

Because for years, we were measured by the mission. Now, we're measured by things like job titles, credit scores, or how well we're "adjusting." But what no one tells you is that adjusting often feels like pretending.

Pretending you're fine.

Pretending you understand how this world works.

Pretending you don't miss the purpose that made you feel alive.

The danger of the identity void isn't just feeling lost; it's staying lost long enough that you forget you ever had direction in the first place. But here's what I've learned: Your rank never defined you. Your uniform never made you who you are. It just amplified the mission already written on your heart.

You were a leader before the army gave you a rank or a title. You were a fighter before you ever carried a weapon. And you are still those things now.

This chapter is about starting the work of remembering who you are—without the name tag and without the orders.

Because rediscovering that identity is the first step to being seen again.

I realized it toward the end of my career, before my last deployment. I had this creeping awareness that my identity wasn't just tied to being a soldier . . . it *was* being a soldier.

Once I retired, I missed the brotherhood. The honor. The pride of walking tall in a uniform that meant something.

When I took it off and no one recognized what it had cost me . . . I felt invisible. And yeah, I was bitter for a while.

Here's what I'd go back and tell myself during those early days of identity loss: *It's okay.*

Just like money or rank, your military service is a tool. It's a launching point; it is not your full identity. Yes, you're going to have to learn how to talk about yourself without sounding like a self-absorbed douchebag. Yes, you'll feel awkward trying to "sell yourself" at first. But you're not a product. You're a person. And when you find the right people—the right tribe, the right opportunity, the right why—they'll see your worth.

You just have to see it first.

Reflection and Recon

- When did you first realize your identity was deeply tied to your military service?
- What specific parts of being a soldier felt like they *were* you?
- What did it feel like the first time someone didn't see "the soldier" in you anymore?
- Have you experienced bitterness or anger that civilians didn't understand what you brought to the table?
- What lies did you start believing about yourself after the transition?
- What helped you begin to reconnect with your sense of worth outside the uniform?
- If you could go back and talk to yourself during that season of identity loss, what would you say?

Call to Action: Reclaim the Mission

Tonight, before your head hits the pillow, grab a pen and write this sentence at the top of a blank page: "This is who I am now." Then, underneath it, list five truths about yourself. No rank. No résumé. No BS.

Write who you are—not who you were. Examples:

- I lead from the front, even without a title.
- I make people better when I'm around them.
- I stay calm under pressure.
- I value honor more than attention.
- I show up.

And if that feels too hard right now—start here instead: "This is who I'm not."

- I'm not broken.
- I'm not worthless.
- I'm not done.
- I'm not invisible.
- I'm not defined by my job or by the rank I left behind.

Sometimes knowing what you aren't is the first step to remembering what you *are*.

When you're done, fold the paper and carry it in your wallet, journal, or glove box for the next thirty days. Read it whenever you start to question your value.

You were never the uniform. You were the fire underneath it. And that fire? It still burns.

CHAPTER 2

LOST IN TRANSLATION

The skills are there. The world just doesn't speak your language.

My Story: The Long Road to a New Career

I was serious about ensuring I was able to provide for my family after I took off my uniform. I applied to and was accepted into Michigan State University's Master of Arts in Criminal Justice program. I wrote résumés and cover letters. I applied to the FBI, NSA, and CIA as well as police departments all across the country. I researched interview techniques and read self-improvement and psychology books and articles. I listened to podcasts on first responders, knowing that they share a lot of the same issues regarding trauma and difficulties processing it.

Things shook out in the wash as they do, and the path forward was the Michigan State Police (MSP). In my opinion, there is not a more professional law enforcement agency in the country than the MSP. I have a lot of love and respect for the NYPD and the LAPD and strongly considered both, but to me, the MSP is just a cut above everyone else.

The interviews were professional and in depth. I flew from North Carolina to Michigan to take the written exam and scored very well. I flew back again later to take their physical fitness test. I did very well on that too. I did my psych eval and my background check, got my physical done, and did more PT tests. All things considered, I was crushing it and was just waiting for my academy date.

Before the military, I wanted to be a cop, so despite that feeling of floating listlessly after retirement, I was eager for what was next. But because of academy schedules and COVID delays, I was stuck in a six-month limbo with no clear path forward.

Upon starting terminal leave in October 2020, I still didn't know my academy start date, so I got a job working security at night to make some extra money. It was a job I didn't care much about, something I'd picked up just to stay busy, not because I believed in it. But it was something to give me a sense of purpose, the flicker of a new identity. I worked there for four months before receiving my academy acceptance letter and reporting to the MSP academy in March 2021.

The academy is an intense, paramilitary environment where candidates live at the academy during the week and return home over the weekend. It's essentially basic training/boot camp all over again. Men shave their heads. You report in a suit with all the stuff on the checklist they send you. You are checked in, marched to your room, and given a crash course of the rules for room standards, cleaning the latrine, taking a shower, and chow. You're constantly being corrected, told you're doing things wrong, etc. It's everything you think of when you think of boot camp or basic training, except you are in a dorm room instead of a bay with bunk beds.

I thought I was ready for the academy. I had done a good job getting into and maintaining the level of fitness I knew would be expected, which was evident on day one when I crushed my PT test and swim eval. I knew what the day-to-day would feel like as they helped transform me out of my civilian mindset into a law enforcement professional mindset—the "we before me" mentality.

What I wasn't ready for was the silence after the day was done.

Lights out was at 10 p.m., and wakeup was at 5 a.m. From 10 p.m. until 3 a.m. or 4 a.m., I would lie in my bed and think about what a failure I was. As a man, as a husband, and as a father. I'd survived three combat tours, and here I was again, putting my kids in a position to not know whether I'd be coming home after my shift. Since I was a rookie, there was no way they were going to give me shift preference. Not exactly the image of a present father.

These intrusive thoughts played over and over in my head for hours upon hours every single day for two weeks until I resigned on March 17, 2021. I had been in a funk all day. I sucked on the run in the morning and hadn't eaten much at any meal during the entire week. By lunch, I knew I was going to resign. I made it until the end of the day when it was time for dinner chow and told my cadre. They did their very best to keep me from resigning, but I knew in my heart if I had any shot of being the father I wanted to be—the father my kids deserved—I needed to make a change. I called my friends and told them. They were surprised but supportive. And when I woke up the next morning without a sense of regret, I knew I had done the right thing.

As reassuring as it was to not feel a sense of regret after resigning from the Michigan State Police, that feeling was short-lived as I realized I was now unemployed and needed to figure out how to provide for myself and my family. I was pretty confident though; I had a bachelor's degree, twenty years of experience, awards, and hard and soft skills. Plus, I was pursuing a master's degree. All things considered, I should have been a hot commodity. Unfortunately, nothing could have been further from the truth. By this time, I lived in the Plymouth-Canton area of Michigan, which is nestled right between Detroit and Ann Arbor. I had absolutely no trouble finding jobs that piqued my interest and that I was qualified for.

My résumé was pretty good, but I was still very much a newbie in this facet of life. I was on LinkedIn, Indeed, ZipRecruiter, Monster—you name it. People love to talk about the red tape and the time things take in a bureaucracy like the federal government, but have you applied to a job lately? It's the 2020s. *Nothing* administrative takes more than a day or two, let alone a week or a month, yet there I was, pumping out dozens of applications a day, hundreds a week. After two weeks of absolute radio silence, I was growing impatient and concerned. I hadn't received an email or a phone call from a single job. When I expressed my frustration to my best friend over a phone call, he asked me to send him my résumé. He and I have the same retirement date, and he'd told me how good of an experience he'd had retiring out of Fort Knox, mainly due to a woman named Paula who worked for an organization called USA Cares. He sent my résumé to Paula, who took time to help overhaul it and revamp it. I got a much better product than I'd had before and immediately put it to work.

Two weeks later, barely any nibbles. I'd been unemployed for a month now, and I was growing concerned. My only income was my army retirement check; the VA was still (understandably) backed up due to COVID, and my rating hadn't been finalized, so I wasn't receiving a VA disability check yet.

I had been told my entire military career that my service plus a college degree equaled instant success. I'd been fed the idea that companies would be falling over themselves to hire me, yet I couldn't find a job in Detroit or Ann Arbor. It's not like I had unrealistic expectations—I wasn't looking for seven figures (or even six figures, to be honest), a corner office with a view of Windsor, or anything unreasonable. But somehow, I couldn't buy a response. It started feeling like a twenty-five-pound kettlebell was sitting where my heart should be; there was just a ton of pressure and weight in the middle of my chest all the time. I couldn't tell you what I looked like at the time because the shame and embarrassment were overbearing. After a shower or when I'd brush my teeth, my mind automatically blurred the image looking back at me in the mirror.

I reached out to a couple of my professors at Michigan State, and they encouraged me to expand my job search radius. I'm glad I listened because within a few days, I heard back from the Michigan Senate Police. They were looking for an operations technical analyst, which was a fancy way of saying they needed someone to run their security center and help with analysis. I crushed the interview and was offered the job on the spot. My only reservation was the commute from my house to Lansing, which was over an hour long. But I had explored and exhausted all resources and options in the Metro Detroit area and desperately needed to be gainfully employed.

I ultimately took the job and am so glad I did. The men I worked with at the Michigan Senate Police were all retired law enforcement, either from the police or sheriff's department, and many had been divorced. I mention that because my own marriage was in trouble. I could relate to them, even if it was just trauma-bonding, so it was like having a dozen big brothers to look after me. I thank God to this very day for those fine gentlemen of the Michigan Senate Police sergeants because there is no way I would have survived without their genuine love and care for me.

It was in this season of change that I learned the hard way that it's not *what* you know—it's *who* you know. Networking is paramount when finding and applying for jobs. Additionally, I have learned that the majority of companies are full of shit. They will use bots to post jobs and then hire internally—or, even worse, they won't remove the job posting, so you waste your time preparing your résumé and cover letter for that specific job only to find out it doesn't exist anymore. They claim to care about you and post incredible job descriptions and mission statements . . . and then completely ignore you.

And don't get me started with the HR software! Why do I upload my résumé at the very beginning of the application process and then have to manually enter that exact same information again over the next several application steps?

Much like a teenager playing *Call of Duty* who gets smoked by a camper several times in an online battle, I crashed out (as the kids say these days) and rage quit dozens of applications because the company's application process was ancient and inefficient. I strongly considered starting a FeetFinder account, but I have wide Hobbit feet and assumed there wasn't much of an audience for that LOL.

Hindsight being 20/20, I now realize that God was keeping doors shut so I would (eventually) find the doors

He had opened for me. I say "eventually" because I needed to learn patience, learn to seek Him, and learn to rely on His understanding and timing, not mine. I needed to find my value as one of His children and not by my title or job description. If I was going to be the man He was calling me to be, I needed to be humbled. I needed to learn not only how to tell a story but also that I actually have a story worth sharing.

The Veteran Advantage

There's a moment, somewhere between the quiet of the transition and the chaos of trying to find your new place in the world, when you stop asking, *What did I lose?* And you start asking, *What do I still have?*

If you've been out for a while, you might not feel like the answer is much. Or, like me, you know you have a ton to offer but are so frustrated at not being able to find a way to contribute in a meaningful manner.

You ever try explaining what you did in the military . . . and get that blank stare? You know the one.

You say, "I led a platoon in Afghanistan," and they say, "Oh cool. So, like, management?" You mention "mass casualty response," and they ask if you're trained in CPR. You put team leader or operations sergeant on a résumé and get told you're underqualified for a job that requires "conflict resolution experience."

Conflict resolution? Bruh, I've de-escalated intense, irrational screaming matches between foreign nationals over the most obscure things that would make WWE script writers nervous.

Maybe you've applied for jobs you knew you could crush but didn't even get an email back. Maybe you've been told you're "overqualified" or "not a cultural fit." Maybe you've started believing the lie that your best years are behind you. But here's what I need you to hear:

You are not at a disadvantage because you're a veteran. You've just been led to believe that.

The truth? You've been pressure-tested. You've led in chaos. You've executed under stress with limited time, limited resources, and zero margin for error. That doesn't make you less valuable in the civilian world. It makes you dangerous—in the best way.

You know how to build trust across cultures. You know how to lead people who don't always want to be led. You know how to manage risk, hold standards, and deliver results when it matters most. That's not just transferable—that's invaluable.

But if you don't recognize it . . . you won't use it. And if you don't learn how to speak about it in a language the world understands, they'll never see it.

The reality is that veterans leave the military with more leadership, crisis management, and adaptability experience than most civilians will ever see. But we enter a job market that doesn't know how to read us. Our language doesn't match theirs.

And so we get filtered out. Passed over. Misunderstood.

The hard part isn't just the job search. It's what that repeated rejection starts to do to you. You begin to question your worth. You start thinking maybe you're not as valuable as you thought. That maybe your experience only mattered over there.

But here's the truth: The world doesn't need to change your past. You need to change how you translate it.

You weren't "just" a team/squad/section/platoon leader. You were never "just" anything. You were responsible for team performance, conflict resolution, logistics, safety, morale, and operational execution in high-risk environments. That's a management degree earned under fire.

You weren't "just" deployed. You lived in a foreign country, collaborated with international forces, adapted daily under pressure, and delivered results with limited resources. That's global leadership.

The problem isn't our skill set; it's that no one ever taught us how to market it.

And on the flip side—let's be honest—most of us weren't exactly trained to ask for help. We weren't taught how to network or tailor a résumé. We were trained to get the job done, not to talk about ourselves.

So, when we transition, we carry all this valuable experience . . . but we bury it under silence, pride, or frustration. And the world misses out on what we bring to the table. This chapter is about closing that gap. Because the day you learn how to speak their language—while staying true to your story—is the day you stop feeling like an outsider and start becoming an asset.

This chapter isn't about fluff. It's not about ego. It's about reclaiming what you've earned—not just in ribbons or rank but in resilience, wisdom, and grit.

You didn't leave your value behind at the gate. It's still with you. It's *in* you.

Now let's talk about how to use it—intentionally, unapologetically, and with impact.

Real Strength Never Needed a Résumé

There was a time I thought I was behind. No corporate title. No six-figure income. No MBA. Just twenty years of leading soldiers and making decisions that actually mattered. But the deeper I got into the civilian world, the more I realized something—I had tools no classroom could teach:

- Integrity.
- Resilience.
- Leadership—real leadership.
- Experience planning, organizing, building teams.
- A commitment to never quitting, never leaving a fallen comrade.
- Cultural awareness from traveling the world and working with people from all walks of life.

The things I once thought made me "different" actually made me dangerous—in the best way.

Speaking a Language They Didn't Understand

When I first entered the civilian world, it felt like stepping onto another planet. Everything I had built—twenty years of leadership, service, sacrifice—suddenly didn't make sense to anyone else.

Trying to explain what you did in the military on two pages of a résumé is insane. There's no bullet point for "responsible for human lives under enemy fire." There's no neat summary for "led warriors into combat and brought them home."

All civilians wanted to hear about was what they saw on TV. My best friend ran SRT/SWAT teams, oversaw high-risk missions . . . but what caught people's attention?

"Oh, you worked crime scenes? Like *CSI*?!"

It was just a small part of his career. But that's what they could connect to. And that's what made the rest of it invisible. Underestimated and misunderstood.

For nine months, I fought like hell to find a job. On paper, I should've been gold—college degree, nearly finished with a master's, decades of leadership experience.

Instead? Ghosted. Dismissed. Overlooked.

I wasn't "marketable." I was a risk they didn't know how to categorize.

And when the emotions cracked through the surface—when I showed anything beyond calm—people didn't see a man. They saw a label.

Too much sympathy, like I was a stray dog. Or fear, like I was unstable or ready to snap. I was neither. I was just a human being—one with good days and bad days. But when I had a bad day? People got nervous.

And nothing angered me more than hearing someone casually say, "I've got PTSD from math class."

No. You don't.

PTSD isn't a punchline. It's not something to trend on TikTok. It's a wound that leaves some of us unable to leave the house, unable to hold jobs, unable to hold on to family.

Casual language waters down serious sacrifice. And veterans carry enough already.

What Civilians Don't Understand (But Need To)

The biggest thing civilians miss about veterans? Purpose.

When we were in uniform, our purpose was crystal clear. It was drilled into us from day one. If you want to unlock a veteran's potential, don't give them fluff. Give them clarity:

- Clear expectations.
- A defined goal.
- The freedom to execute.

That's it. Skip the corporate jargon. Don't micromanage. Don't second-guess the approach if the result is solid.

Unless you're solving for math or surgery, the "how" is flexible. And if a veteran finds purpose in their civilian work? Watch out. They will move mountains.

When Doubt Creeps In . . . And How I Found My Way Back

There were days when I truly believed I didn't belong in this world outside the military or law enforcement. *You're not cut out for this. You're a burden. Just go be a cop—that's all you're really made for.*

Imposter syndrome doesn't whisper—it roars.

What saved me wasn't the system. It wasn't the process. It was the people who saw me.

My family.

My pastor and life coach.

My coworkers at the Michigan Senate—retired cops who got it.

My players and fellow coaches at Hillsdale College, at St. Frances Cabrini High School, and on the Michigan Monarchs.

They made me feel respected. Welcomed. Loved. And they still do.

None of them needed to hear war stories to believe in me. They saw something deeper. They didn't see a veteran's résumé. They saw a man with purpose. They saw a coach. A servant. A leader who still had something to give.

They reminded me that my time in the army wasn't a full stop. It was a launching pad. And slowly, I started to believe it too. Not because I suddenly "fit in." But because I remembered who I really was underneath the uniform.

A son of God.

A man called to serve.

A mentor. A father. A teacher. A builder.

And the moment I shifted from proving my worth to living it through serving others—everything changed.

What I Would Tell You

If you're feeling unseen right now, listen: I see you. I don't know your exact story. I don't know every mile you've walked.

But I know this: The world is better with you in it. Life is a team sport—find yourself a few good teammates and never let them go. It's not easy. But it's worth it.

You are not invisible. You are not alone.

You are not done.

Reflection and Recon

- When was the first time you realized civilians didn't really understand your experience? How did it make you feel to try to explain it—and be met with confusion or indifference?
- What doubts started whispering in your mind after the transition?
- Who—if anyone—has truly *seen you* since you left the uniform behind?
- What strength have you been downplaying that's actually your superpower?
- What purpose would you chase today if you believed you were already equipped for it?

Call to Action: Redefine Your Story

Take five minutes tonight. On one side of a piece of paper, write down the military titles or roles you used to define yourself by (e.g., platoon sergeant, squad leader, intelligence analyst, medic, etc.).

Then, flip the paper over. Write the human identities that still exist underneath:

- Leader.
- Mentor.
- Protector.
- Teacher.
- Builder.
- Coach.
- Fighter.

Your value was never in the title. It was in the fire that carried you through it.

Now, make a list with two columns:

- Left side: Military skills (e.g., squad leader, convoy ops, operations planning).
- Right side: Civilian strengths those translate into (e.g., project management, logistics, team development).

Then do two things:

- Use it as a confidence check. This is your real résumé.
- Pick one item and lead with it this week in your work, family, or community.

You are not "behind." You are not "less than." You are not lost in translation. You are being revealed—one real word, one real action, one real day at a time. And the world needs to hear you speak your truth again.

CHAPTER 3

THE SILENT STRUGGLE

It's not that they don't care. It's that they don't know what you're carrying.

My Story: A Family Fractured

Much like when a hurricane devastates a coastal town, I should have seen it coming, but I ignored the warning signs. The divorce didn't just happen out of nowhere; in fact, I realized after my ex-wife uttered those infamous words that the signs had started about fourteen months prior.

I was on my final deployment, a noncombat deployment to support the United States Army Europe (USAREUR) and our allies across the European theater. I had volunteered for the deployment, although it *had* been sold to me in a different capacity. It had been eight years since I last deployed, and I figured it was time for me to pull my weight again.

Saying goodbye to my wife and kids was startlingly more difficult this time than it had ever been. Ty was twelve, and Juliana was ten; they were no longer oblivious little kids. They knew full well I was leaving but couldn't fully comprehend why.

I got to the unit well before we were required to, sat in my truck, and cried. Unbeknownst to me at the time, that would be the last time I cried for fifty-seven months.

I started the deployment at the Novo Selo Training Area in Bulgaria. That portion of my rotation lasted three months, and I rejoined the main element in Poznań, Poland, on Fourth of July weekend.

I hadn't been back in Poland for more than a day or two when I got a cryptic message on Facebook from my wife. I excused myself from the cold, concrete-walled, dirt-floored room we called our office and found a place where I had decent Wi-Fi connectivity so I could call her.

She was in Michigan with her family; they were doing their annual summer family trip up north. She was upset that I was going to miss her sister's wedding. She was still highly irritated that I had volunteered for the deployment and was struggling with the kids, who were, for the first time, old enough to experience the negative emotions that come when Dad is deployed. It was a lot, and she had every right to be upset.

She used terminology that hinted, suggested, and implied that she was considering divorce, but I talked her down and thought I put those worries to rest. Hell, that time the following year, we'd be packing up the house and getting ready to move to wherever we decided to build our future lives. Things were relatively better until Christmastime. We got into a huge fight on Christmas Eve, then barely spoke to each other on Christmas Day.

I got home from deployment in mid-February 2020, right as COVID-19 took hold of the entire globe. There was a palpable distance from her, a distinct lack of affection. She kept needing time away from me and the kids. I attributed it to a long, emotionally draining deployment coupled with the uncertainty of the effects of COVID and what life after the military would look like. All understandable.

During one spat, she told me I had "let myself go," which I found odd, as I had hit the gym hard while deployed and came back in pretty decent shape. I'd even secured a spot in the Arnold Classic Europe amateur division for functional fitness, placing thirtieth out of thirty spots. I'd had to decline the event, as I came home on emergency leave due to my wife needing surgery at the same time the event was to occur.

Hearing her concern and wanting to show I cared, I became a gym rat. I ran or rucked every morning and hit the gym every day. I was doing 75 Hard before it was a thing. Even when the state of North Carolina finally conceded and shut down for a couple of months, I found a nearby renegade gym and worked out there. At thirty-nine, I looked and felt better than I had in well over a decade.

Nonetheless, the spats turned into full-fledged arguments, which grew in both intensity and frequency. I remember sitting in my truck one day and calling my dad, confessing to him I was worried we weren't going to make it. I remained defiantly optimistic though. We'd weathered far worse before; we could make it through this. Hell, we were going to be completely free from the military lifestyle in just a few months.

My wife had taken a couple of short trips to Michigan to visit her parents early on after I returned from deployment, and after one trip, she announced we were moving to Michigan. I was taken aback, as she'd never shown interest in living in Michigan. In fact, she'd been adamant for most of our marriage that moving back to Michigan was not a consideration.

Upon hearing her announcement, I was ecstatic. I've always loved Michigan and considered it home, having lived there two separate times for three years each. We both had family there, and the schools were great—this seemed like an absolute win.

But the startling announcements weren't over. She declared in April that she had always wanted to work in a big city and had found a job in Detroit. It was the first time I recalled ever hearing that dream, but after over nineteen years in the army, I had very little to stand on; she had supported me at every duty station, deployment, training exercise, and schooling opportunity. The least I could do was be supportive and encourage her.

She ended up getting hired and moved in with her parents in Michigan in May. The kids would join her in the summer, and I would follow in the fall. It would suck a little bit that she was going to be gone, but she had earned it. Being a stay-at-home mom and a military spouse is not for the faint of heart. She deserved to get situated and figure out her new role in corporate America, and she'd have the chance to do some recon on where we'd live. There's nothing wrong with a little short-term pain for long-term gain, right?

The housing market in the summer of 2020 was still a seller's market, so we decided to find something to rent for a year, get our bearings, and really understand the house-buying process before we settled on a place to live. We'd only ever lived on base except for a few places we'd rented. This was a smart move. She found a great townhome that was in a brand-new community, in our price range, a few minutes from her parents' house, and a forty-five-minute drive from my brothers' place. This would be great.

In July, when I drove the kids up, we bought a lot of new furniture. A new couch, a new entertainment center, new bedroom sets for us and the kids. Things were looking up. Even though COVID-19 policies were still in effect, and I essentially had no job, I couldn't stay in Michigan, or else I would be AWOL. So, I'd travel back and forth every few weeks and help out where I could. We got our household goods delivered in September, and I found a storage facility to hold the stuff we didn't need in the rental. We were only going to be there for a year, after all.

During that trip, we attended an engagement party for a friend of a friend. My wife and I got into a heated argument in the first few moments we were in the truck heading back to the house. We did not speak for the entirety of the remaining hourlong drive back home. Things were not much better the next morning, so I packed up my stuff and drove back to North Carolina a day early, despite the guilt trips being thrust upon me about leaving the kids to go back to my "precious army." I literally didn't feel like staying one more night in a place where I didn't feel welcome, let alone loved.

I only had three more weeks left in the army when I got back to North Carolina. The lease on the house we rented in the lake community was up, so I was staying with a close friend in his guest room. The texts and calls got shorter and more venomous from both of us. My last day in uniform was supposed to be September 30, 2020. However, due to a clerical error at the G-1 level (the army equivalent of HR at the corporate level), the leave (vacation days) I had accrued was off by two, and my last day would be Friday, October 2.

That morning, my phone rang. I stepped outside and took the call in my truck, which was parked along the street outside my friend's house. I did not want to admit it at the time, but I knew what the call was, which is why I took it outside. I wanted the privacy to fall apart if I needed to. Then she uttered the words that shattered my entire existence: "I want a divorce."

I've had some nasty hangovers in my day. I got the Iraqi crud in 2004. I got the Afghan flu in 2010, and it took me out of the fight for two whole days. But I had never felt as sick as I did when I heard those words. Again, like a coastal townie who didn't see the signs, I was absolutely blindsided by a Category 5 hurricane with landfall occurring right on my heart. I went silent—I have no idea for how long. I could feel the bile climbing up the back of my throat, and my salivary glands were working overtime in my mouth. I was a volcano about to erupt. My hands gripped the steering wheel like I was trying to strangle the life out of it.

Somehow, we navigated the rest of the conversation. I was pretty much in shock and don't remember much. We agreed to speak later regarding how things would work out once I moved to Michigan in a few days. Later that night, I discovered that Michigan does not require a separation period before filing for divorce. I flat-out told her that I did not support the divorce and that if she was serious about it, she was going to have to pay for it and file for it; I wanted nothing to do with the dissolution of our marriage.

We both agreed that I had nowhere else to live and that this was a bombshell to drop on the kids, so I would stay at the townhouse with them. But with the crumbling of my marriage, the chasm between me and the ones I loved most yawned wider than ever before. The silence only grew, and I faded further to the point that I didn't just feel invisible—I felt like life had stopped.

When the Homefront Becomes the Battlefield

There's this idea that once you're home, the hardest part is over. The danger's gone. The bags are unpacked. The boots are off. But for a lot of veterans, home is where the quietest battle begins.

You're back in your house—but you don't feel like you belong in it. You're surrounded by people you love—but something's off. You don't sleep well. You're tense at the sound of a slammed door or a glass breaking. You withdraw, sometimes without even realizing it.

And your spouse? Your kids? They want to help—but they don't know how. You're quieter than you used to be. Maybe angrier. More tired.

They don't ask what's wrong because, frankly, they don't want to say the wrong thing. And you don't explain—because you've been trained not to complain.

You tell yourself: *They didn't deploy. They wouldn't understand anyway*. So you stay quiet. You white-knuckle through it.

And the people closest to you . . . start to feel further and further away. That's how the struggle becomes silent—dangerously so.

I lived this. I came home with a wall built around me. I didn't mean to. I wasn't trying to push anyone away. But after two decades of being the strong one—the one with the answers, the one who kept others safe—I didn't know how to let anyone in.

And that's how, during that first stretch of my transition, I lost my marriage.

As you just read, it wasn't sudden. It wasn't dramatic. It was the slow unraveling of connection that comes when you don't know how to share the weight of what you've seen and who you've become.

When no one asks what you're carrying . . . and you don't offer it.

Here's the hard truth: Veterans don't always know how to ask for help. And families don't always know how to give it.

But that doesn't mean there's no hope. It means we need a shared language. It means we need to stop pretending we're fine when we're not. It means we need to give our people a chance to see us, not just salute our past. The silent struggle becomes survivable when we stop trying to carry it alone.

The goal of this chapter isn't to assign blame—it's to build bridges. Because reconnecting with your people doesn't require perfect words. It requires presence. Honesty, humility, transparency, and vulnerability. And the courage to speak—even when your voice shakes.

My Story: From Broken to Building

I'd gotten a job with UPS on first shift, so I'd be gone from 2 a.m. to 7 a.m., which meant she could get ready for work in peace and I could be present during the day with the kids. They still had fairly early bedtimes, with TVs and video games in their rooms, so chances were they'd be oblivious to the gravity of the situation of Mom in the bedroom and me staying in the living room.

I got a much better-paying, nonunion job doing corporate security on the night shift in October. That made things way easier. There was very little overlap in our schedules. I'd get home shortly before she went to work. Then I could sleep in a bed as opposed to on the couch during the day, but I was still available if the kids needed me. I'd get home around 7 a.m., hang out with the kids till school started an hour later, and fall asleep around 9 or 10 a.m. I'd get up at 2 p.m., make sure school was good and tend to any of the kids' needs, and then hit the gym or go for a run. I was still in the Michigan State Police Academy pipeline and needed to be ready. My schedule at work was awesome. We worked ten-hour shifts with the option for overtime almost every day. I took it as much as I could. We did a 4:3 schedule—four days on followed by three days off.

Interactions with my "wife" were few and far between, characterized by a polite disdain for each other. Inside, I was furious. How was this woman willing to throw away seventeen years of marriage?

Thanksgiving and Christmas sucked. She and the kids were spending the holidays with her family, so I volunteered to work overtime. Fuck it—I was a stranger in my own home anyways. I slept on a couch (which my paratrooper neck, back, and knees loved . . . sarcastic eye roll) in the house I was paying rent for. I had to knock to enter the bedroom where my closet and dresser were. I was a nuisance, a mosquito at a barbecue, just irritating the life out of people there. Cool.

I gave my wife everything she wanted. She notified me that she'd officially filed for divorce. Right before going to Florida for Christmas, she tearfully explained to me how worried she was that when they returned, she was going to find all her belongings on the street. I was incensed that she would think I was capable of that, but I calmed myself and explained to her that there was no way I would do that. We had been fairly amicable in the divorce decision-making process, and I would honor and uphold my end. When they returned, I was true to my word and, in fact, had tidied up her bedroom just to be nice.

I need to clarify something here: In every relationship, it takes two. I was no saint, no angel. I could have and should have been a much better husband. I am as much to blame, if not more so, for the divorce; she just had the balls to call it off. Intrinsically, I took a lot of things for granted, maybe nothing more so than time, when I irrationally determined that things would be hunky-dory once I retired.

In April, she found a house down the road and bought it. We still had two full months left on the lease, but hey, that was my problem. On the weekends and some weeknights, she and her parents and the kids would go over and paint, update lights, etc. One Saturday, I even dropped off Burger King for lunch for all of them.

She moved out of the townhome sometime in late April or early May. I didn't fight for anything. All of the new furniture—she got it. The good TV? She got it. The pots, pans, silverware, dishes, and cups? She got it all. I'm such a sucker that when the movers were taking their sweet time moving the furniture into her new house, I joined them and outworked them because they were charging her by the hour. That was literally the only time I ever set foot inside her house. Every kid swap, I stayed outside. I would hand suitcases through the door. I refused to go in.

So, now, it was just me in the townhome. I still have the picture of my living room in the aftermath on my phone. My entertainment center was two black-and-yellow storage boxes from Costco stacked on top of each other. I had a thirty-two-inch TV on top of it. I had a collapsible folding chair for a couch. I didn't buy a mattress for weeks; the carpet in the bedroom was new, so it was soft and plush. Plus, I'd slept on and in far worse while deployed. Eventually, I got a sweet deal on a king-size mattress from Costco, I think during their Memorial Day sale. The house echoed constantly because there was no art, no pictures, nothing on the walls. It was as sterile as a hospital operating room—and so was my heart.

The timing of our separation and subsequent divorce felt intentional and cruel. I was transitioning from the army. I loved being a soldier, and I was struggling severely with my loss of identity. Hindsight being 20/20, I think God allowed both of these blows to happen simultaneously because there's no way I would have survived if they happened in different phases or at separate times.

At the time, it felt like complete destruction. I did not know yet that it was also the beginning of a rebuilding I never would have chosen but desperately needed.

The Power of the Pause

One of the hardest lessons I've had to learn after retirement is this: Authenticity and vulnerability matter most with the people who know you best. Especially your family.

For years, I believed strength meant control. *Hold it together. Push through. Handle it quietly.* That mindset works in uniform. At home, it creates distance.

What I've learned since is that leadership doesn't disappear when the uniform comes off, but it does require a different tempo. Sometimes the strongest move isn't action. It's a pause.

One of the most impactful lessons I've learned in my transition is the importance of intentionally pausing to focus on a specific role or season of life. Not quitting. Not retreating. Pausing with purpose.

For most of our careers, we're conditioned to do everything at once. Lead the team. Get the mission done. Take care of the family. Prepare for what's next. That pace is necessary in uniform. During transition, it becomes unsustainable.

The pause creates clarity, and clarity leads to better decisions.

When everything feels urgent, nothing gets the attention it deserves. We start reacting instead of choosing. We spread ourselves thin and call it discipline, when in reality, it's exhaustion wearing a badge of honor.

Here's the truth many veterans need to hear: You can have it all—just not all right now.

That isn't failure. That's prioritization.

Different seasons require different focuses. Sometimes the mission is your career. Sometimes it's healing. Sometimes it's rebuilding trust at home. The mistake is trying to fight every battle simultaneously and wondering why nothing feels steady.

A pause doesn't mean you're giving something up forever. It means you're choosing what matters most right now. You're saying, "This season deserves my full attention."

That kind of focus is not weakness. It's mature leadership.

Veterans understand this intuitively in combat and operations. You don't clear an entire city at once. You clear a room. Then a hallway. Then the next objective. You move with intention, not impatience.

Life after service works the same way.

If your family is strained, the pause may mean your career momentum slows while you rebuild connection. If your identity feels shaken, the pause may mean focusing inward before charging ahead. If everything feels fractured, the pause gives you space to breathe, assess, and choose wisely.

This is how progress is actually made. Not by doing more but by doing the right thing at the right time.

When you pause with purpose, you stop chasing everything and start engaging with what matters. And that's when momentum returns—not all at once but steadily and sustainably.

You can have it all in this next chapter of life. Just not all at the same time.

Veterans are wired to think long term. Big picture. Next mission. Next phase. But family life after service isn't about the five-year plan. It's about the fifty-meter target right in front of you.

Handle what's closest. Engage it fully. Knock it down. Then reassess and move forward.

One of my favorite leadership stories comes from a drill Command Sergeant Major (CSM) J. D. Pendry, author of *The Three Meter Zone: Common Sense Leadership for NCOs*, once ran with his soldiers. He would blindfold them and place two quarters in the room. Those quarters represented threats. One was placed several feet away, sometimes off to the side. The other was placed right in front of the soldier's boot.

When the blindfold came off, every time, the soldier saw the quarter farthest away first. Not once did they notice the one at their feet.

The lesson was simple and brutal: The closest threat is usually right in front of you, but we miss it because we're focused on something else.

After retirement, that "threat" is rarely dramatic. It's the conversation you're avoiding. The tension you're pretending not to feel. The emotional distance growing quietly between you and the people you love.

We look ahead to career moves, financial stability, the next goal, the next win. Meanwhile, the most important target is sitting right at our feet, asking for attention.

Rebuilding connection with your family doesn't start with fixing everything. It starts with awareness. With slowing down long enough to see what's right in front of you. With choosing presence over projection.

You don't need to solve your entire life today. You need to engage the next right thing. One honest conversation. One moment of listening. One act of vulnerability.

I'll say it again: That is not weakness. That is disciplined leadership in unfamiliar terrain.

Getting Honest with Yourself

I want you to think about the most important, dangerous, or significant mission you ever prepared for. Did you approach it haphazardly? No. You did a map recon; you talked to the S-2 to get intel on known and named areas of interest. You identified the landowner and confirmed their call signs and frequencies. You prepared an operation order (OPORD) or attended a mission brief. You performed weapons and vehicle maintenance, ensured dispatches were signed, and verified trip tickets were accurate and submitted correctly. You conducted pre-combat checks (PCCs) and pre-combat inspections (PCIs). You conducted rehearsals. You ensured everyone and everything going on that mission was good to go.

Your exit from the military is the most important mission you will ever prepare for. I need you to take it as seriously as, if not more so than, any mission you did while in uniform. Because before you can rebuild anything, you have to take stock of where you actually are. Not where you wish you were. Not where you think you should be.

In the military, recon comes before movement. You do not advance blindly. You observe. You assess terrain, threats, strengths, and limitations. You get honest about reality so you can make smart decisions.

Transition requires the same discipline.

Take a moment to reflect on the season you are in right now. Not the one you are chasing, not the one you lost—the one you are living.

This is not about guilt. It is about clarity.

Many veterans pride themselves on endurance. On pushing through. On handling things quietly. But reflection is not weakness; it is situational awareness. And situational awareness is what keeps you alive in unfamiliar environments.

You do not need to relive everything. You do not need to fix everything. You just need to notice what is actually happening around you and inside you.

Because you cannot lead what you refuse to acknowledge.

Recon is quiet. It is deliberate. It is honest. And it sets the conditions for progress. You remember the six "Ps": **P**rior **p**lanning **p**revents **p**iss **p**oor **p**erformance.

Reflection and Recon

- Where am I withdrawing instead of engaging?
- What conversations am I avoiding because they feel uncomfortable or unfamiliar?
- What am I carrying that no one else knows about?
- Who is closest to me, and how present am I really being with them?

Call to Action: Pause with Purpose

For the next seven days, practice one deliberate pause each day. Not a break. Not a distraction. A pause with intention.

Choose a consistent time—early morning, late evening, etc.—and go somewhere quiet—in your car, on a walk, wherever is conducive to thoughtful reflection for you.

During that pause, ask yourself three questions and answer them honestly, even if the answers are uncomfortable:

1. What season am I actually in right now?
2. What am I trying to push through that requires patience instead?
3. What is the one area of my life that needs focused attention before anything else?

Do not problem-solve yet. Do not make a plan. Just observe.

Write the answers down in a notebook, on your phone, on a scrap of paper—he medium does not matter. The honesty does.

At the end of the week, look for the pattern. The repeated answer. The thing that keeps showing up.

That is your next objective.

Not your five-year plan. Not your next promotion. Not the thing that looks impressive from the outside. The thing that requires your immediate attention.

Progress after service does not come from speed. It comes from alignment. When you pause with purpose, clarity follows. And clarity creates momentum that lasts.

CHAPTER 4

THE WAR DOESN'T END AT HOME

No one tells you how loud the silence is after war.

My Story: Coping Skills or Avoidance Tactics?

For as long as I can remember, I wanted to be a dad. So going through a divorce was pretty much the worst thing I could experience because it meant I wouldn't get to be around my kids as much. I was lucky enough to walk away from six deployments with all my fingers, toes, limbs, etc., but I would have traded any of those not to be separated from my children.

When it comes to divorce, the system is already stacked against you if you're a man. I've seen it with friends and military buddies and experienced it myself: Just because you have a stable income and are painted as the bad guy, you get raked over the coals. The kids are used as pawns against you. Your flesh and bone, your mini-mes, your DNA duplicates . . . the very reason you made it home from combat and, to be honest, the only thing that kept you alive during your darkest hours are now being manipulated and used to extort money from you. Your fatherhood basically turns into a subscription . . . *"Oh, sure, you can see your kids—for the low price of $1,000 per month."* And that's not even a full-time subscription. If you're LUCKY like me and get 50/50 custody, you're paying $500 a week to see your kids. For others who aren't as fortunate as me, the price goes up and/or the time with their kids goes down. Fathers like me would pay many times over because it's worth getting to be with and take care of their kids, but it is ridiculous how children are weaponized and monetized against the father in divorce proceedings.

As we discussed earlier, I don't really know what the exact catalyst for the divorce was, but I will give my ex-wife credit—we worked through the details of the divorce fairly amicably; we came to agreements on everything without lawyers. Even so, during our hearing, the judge, who was a woman, strongly encouraged my ex-wife to seek more money. When I heard this, I was appalled. I could feel the blood rush to my face as I flushed red with rage, fear, and embarrassment. My molars crunched down on each other as my jaw clenched and my face tightened. I could feel my hands turn clammy with sweat, my pulse increase like a thermometer in the heat of a cartoon, and my peripheral vision start going fuzzy. I thought I was going to pass out. Almost all the same physiological symptoms that happen in the initial seconds of a firefight. I was growing irate.

Lock in, I told myself firmly.

Not only was I paying more than required by the state, but we had agreed on 50/50 joint legal and physical custody, and we lived a mile apart from each other. For all intents and purposes, I was being a pushover. There was no legitimate reason for me to be paying child support.

Fortunately, and to her credit, my ex did not take the judge's bait. She kept her word and stuck to the parameters we had agreed on. I felt an awkward sensation—gratitude. There *was* hope. My heart rate slowed, my jaw loosened, and I could breathe again. I listened as holidays, medical expenses, and even taxes were divvied up like poker chips after a big hand.

Outside of the courtroom, my ex and I eventually figured out the battle rhythm; we would do kid swap on Sunday afternoons. Sundays became an emotional rollercoaster. On the Sundays I had the kids, I could hardly contain myself. I'd clean the house, go to the grocery store, and count down the seconds until they were there. On the days I had to take them back to their mom's, I was like a duck in water. On the surface, I was fine. I had to pretend like it was okay that my world was going to be taken away from me for the next week. It would have been unfair of me to put any more pressure on the kids, whose whole worlds (literally and figuratively) were changing every seven days as well. But underneath the surface, I was going a million miles an hour. My heart rate would climb to well over 150 beats per minute, and I would get so dehydrated because my parasympathetic nervous system would dump adrenaline to keep me alive and conscious, thinking we were in fight-or-flight mode. Leaving my kids had the same physiological effect on me as war.

Unlike in a combat zone, at home, I had access to alcohol. And boy, was alcohol an ever-present and faithful battle buddy. On Sundays, after I dropped the kids off, I would stop by the liquor store on the way home. Or I would park in the driveway and walk over. I lived the distance of a football field from a busy intersection, and on the corner closest to me was a liquor store. I went so often that the owner knew me by name, and we eventually became friends. I would grab a fifth of Jack Daniel's and some Diet Coke, go home, and start self-medicating. Kid swap happened in the midafternoon, so I could get good and drunk and still get enough sleep so I wasn't irresponsible behind the wheel the next morning, which included a commute of an hour to an hour and a half, depending on where I was working at the time.

As I would pour my first drink, I would softly sing the chorus of Toby Keith's "Whiskey Girl" to myself.

> *Just ain't enough good burn in tequila, she needs somethin' with a little more edge and a little more pain.*

I needed something to compete with the pain in my heart, and whiskey sure does the trick, especially if you have a few of them.

Earlier, I mentioned the silence that came with my transition from the military. The weeks I didn't have my kids, I was a mess, and the silence was deafening and dangerous.

After work, I'd try to muscle through the silence, fear, doubt, and insecurities, but because I hadn't built my relationship with God just yet, I lost that battle nine times out of ten. I'd go to the fridge, grab my liquid best friend, and assume my position on the couch. As "the nectar of the gods" did its magic, I would hear and embody the words of Metallica's "One" (one of my all-time favorite songs):

> *Deep down inside, I feel the scream. This terrible silence stops with me. Now that the war is through with me, I'm waking up, I cannot see that there's not much left of me. Nothing is real but pain now.*

Nothing is real but pain now . . . That's the cycle I was stuck in. I didn't know how to properly address my issues, so I took the shortest, easiest route, which was to drown them. Alcohol is a quick-acting medicine, but it has its own side effects. You wake up feeling a little too dry, like your tongue and throat borrowed sandpaper overnight. There's a dull, steady pressure behind the eyes—not a pounding headache, just a reminder that your body's low on water and your sleep quality dipped. Your stomach feels unsettled, almost like it's thinking about being nauseous but hasn't fully committed. Food doesn't sound good yet, but coffee feels like a risk.

Your brain's a half-step slow. Nothing painful, just filled with a fog that makes simple tasks require a beat. You can still function at work, carry on conversations, get through the day—but everything feels slightly out of sync. Lights are a touch brighter, sounds are a bit sharper, and your patience is a little thinner. You're not hungover enough to complain, just hungover enough to know you're not firing on all cylinders.

This became a normal experience for me as I spiraled further into self-isolation and drinking. As a newly divorced, single dad living in my own home for the first time, I saved money where I could. I drank myself to sleep most nights when I didn't have my kids. It didn't matter if it was a Tuesday night, the middle of the week. I wanted to feel something, anything, even if the feeling was just a numb frontal cortex and the blurred vision from that sweet Tennessee goodness.

When It All Fell Quiet

The isolation came almost immediately. It wasn't just retiring from the army. It wasn't just leaving the brotherhood. It was watching my whole life crack at once.

I wasn't just losing my identity as a soldier. I was losing my identity as a husband. And my identity as a father suddenly felt unstable—unclear.

One day, I belonged somewhere. The next day, I was floating. And the silence? It didn't feel peaceful. It felt punishing.

Choosing Isolation—Even When I Didn't Have To

There were moments when I could've reached out. I knew it. But honestly? Some days, I couldn't even look in the mirror. The idea of facing people felt exhausting.

For example, dating again? It was exciting. But it was draining.

"What's your favorite color?"

"What do you do for work?"

"Do you like it?"

Gag me.

It felt like putting on another uniform—this time, with no armor underneath. I much preferred staying home, pouring a couple of drinks, and watching something safe and familiar.

No expectations. No pretending. No conversations that reminded me of what I lost.

At War with Myself

After I retired, I was surrounded by noise—divorce, transition, the kids going back and forth between homes. But inside? It was silent.

And the silence was deafening.

It was not the peaceful kind of silence. It was the kind of quiet that swallows you whole. Where everything slows down on the outside, but inside, you're screaming for direction . . . and no one can hear those cries for help.

I was going through a divorce. Trying to be a father. Trying to be stable when I felt anything but.

I had joint custody of my kids. I lived a mile from their mom. But some days . . . it might as well have been an ocean away. When they left my house, my heart broke. Still does.

In many ways, that's when the real war started. In the silence, the lies got loud.

What you did doesn't matter here.

You're a burden.

You're a fraud.

You peaked in uniform.

I numbed it the way a lot of us do: I self-medicated with alcohol. I doomscrolled endlessly. I smiled through pain when I had to. But inside? I was sinking. I could put on a mask around family, sure. But it drained me. Every time I did, I walked away feeling hollow.

Eventually, I had a panic attack. My sleep fell apart. My gut health did too. I gained weight. I lost direction. And I was consumed by the thought: *Who am I now?*

See, when you're isolated long enough, the lies get louder:

You have to do this alone.

No one else understands.

Don't burden anyone with your problems.

This is your mess. You fix it—or die trying.

And the worst part? Some of those lies sound noble. They sound like strength. But they're chains. They isolate you not just from others—but from yourself.

The truth is veterans face a unique battle: Divorce. Substance abuse. Identity crisis. Isolation.

You're not imagining it. You're living it.

When Something Finally Broke Through

It's going to sound silly, but you know what cracked the wall for me?

Ted Lasso.

Yeah, a TV show. I binge-watched the first two seasons in a weekend. And for the first time in months, something hit me: I wasn't crazy. I wasn't broken beyond repair. I was human.

Ted wasn't perfect. He struggled. He hurt. He carried silent battles behind that easy smile.

And somehow, seeing that play out—honestly, vulnerably—made me realize I'm not alone; I'm just hurt. And that's not the same thing as broken.

The Illusion of Isolation

One of the cruelest tricks of transition is the lie that you're the only one going through it. No one says it out loud—but the silence of others makes it feel true.

You scroll through social media, and it looks like every other veteran has it figured out. New job. Happy family. Killer physique. Big smiles.

Meanwhile, you're sitting in your truck outside a VA appointment, wondering why you feel like a stranger in your own life.

Those around you don't see the thousand-yard stare behind your smile. They don't see the nights you drank too much just to be able to sleep. They don't see the therapy appointments, the near-breakdowns, or the daily struggle to believe you still matter.

You're not alone. You've just been isolated by a culture that taught you that suffering in silence is strength.

But silence isn't strength. Silence is what keeps us stuck.

The truth is there are thousands of us walking around every day—functioning, yes, but fighting ghosts in the quiet moments. Carrying guilt for surviving. Missing the camaraderie more than we can explain. Trying to be "normal," even though the things we've seen will never let us go back to what normal used to mean.

Here's the good news: That illusion of isolation starts to fade the moment you speak honestly to another veteran. The moment you say, "Man, this is harder than I expected," and they reply, "Yeah. Me too." The moment you share your story and someone nods—not out of politeness but because they've lived it.

That connection? That shared language? That's the beginning of healing. It's what the uniform gave us—but it doesn't end when we take it off.

You were never meant to fight this alone. And the second you realize that, you start to reclaim your power.

So if you've been waiting for a sign to reach out—to a battle buddy, a mentor, a counselor, a support group—this is it.

Because isolation is a liar. And connection . . . is the way back.

My Story: My Kids, My Lifeline

I love being a dad; it is the most fulfilling and rewarding thing I have ever done and will ever do. My kids are my world. They kept me alive more times than I care to admit. That's what made the divorce suck so bad. I know plenty of parents—mothers and fathers alike—who can't wait until their kid moves away. Not me. I want to be involved in everything. I want my kids around as much as possible for as long as they can stand it. I want them to come home from college and do laundry, eat up all the food, nap on the couch, and sleep in too late.

When they come home, they don't knock; they just come right in. They get the dogs riled up, and Shadow (my mountain cur) pees as soon as she recognizes them. I never want this to change. And it won't end after college. Wherever they are, wherever I am, I want them to know, beyond the shadow of a doubt, that they are loved and welcome home anytime they want—and then some.

There was no typical day with my kids, as we tried to make every day an adventure. Obviously, that was difficult with work and school, so we tried to take advantage of our Saturdays, as they would go back to their mom's house on

Sundays. I wanted days like this to prove to them—and maybe to myself—that even though everything else was changing, our time together was still sacred.

One of my favorite Saturdays was November 13, 2021. We'd just had our first snowfall a few days before, and it was already midwinter cold in Michigan. That Saturday, the kids and I decided we were going to break the societal norm of waiting until Thanksgiving to decorate for Christmas. During the divorce, I'd given my ex damn near everything in the house. The cool thing about that meant I was starting from scratch with a clean slate. There was no template, just a bare canvas for us to do what we wanted.

The kids and I jumped in the car and went to Target. We spent a few hundred dollars on ornaments, decorations, lights, etc., but when we got home, we realized we had barely scratched the surface and needed more. A *lot* more.

So we got back in the car and drove two hours north to Frankenmuth, a town very German in its roots, design, architecture, and culture. People really only go there for two reasons. The first is to get an authentic German chicken dinner from Zehnder's or the Bavarian Inn. The second is to go to Bronner's Christmas Wonderland, the self-proclaimed "World's Largest Christmas Store." We couldn't get our chicken dinner because this was a spur-of-the-moment trip, and that time of year, you needed reservations, especially on a Saturday night. Bronner's, on the other hand, required only intestinal fortitude for willingly stepping into the thunderdome of holiday season shopping.

I found a parking spot fairly close to one of the entrances, and we made a beeline to the line to get in. Ty was wearing one of my softball hoodies. Juliana had on leggings, Uggs, and a fashionable white, fuzzy sweater. I was wearing jeans, Chelsea boots, a green sweater, and a dark brown, *Yellowstone*-style cowboy jacket. The air was cold, and the wind was getting aggressive. I was worried if we were outside very long, the kids were going to be miserable. Luckily, we only had to wait in line for about ten minutes. As we crossed the threshold of the heavy oak doors, the warm air, which was scented with cinnamon, embraced us like an old friend. We grabbed a shopping cart and went to work.

Bronner's is about the size of a Walmart Supercenter and is broken into sections. I hadn't been there since I was a kid in the nineties, and my son and daughter had never been. So I resisted the military urge to make this efficient. I wanted to indulge in the Christmas spirit, wanted the kids to immerse themselves in the controlled chaos that is shopping at Bronner's during the holiday season.

We perused every. Single. Shelf. We performed delicate ballets in and around aisles with other shoppers. We laughed at the creative and eclectic decorations. We looked intently at and admired the handcrafted ornaments and figurines. By the end of our time there, we had each found a handful of ornaments: a macaroni and cheese one for

Ty and beautiful glass grapes as well as a fun sushi roll for Juliana. I found some cool military ornaments. Then we found our tree. It was a six-foot pre-lit tree, and I paid way too much for it, but it was ours. We also picked out another tree to put in the kitchen and found some simple blue and silver ornaments to decorate it with.

As we continued to wend our way through the Christmas wonderland, we paused to snag a nice ceramic nativity set and a beautiful handmade wooden barn to place the scene in. We found some small pre-lit decorative pine trees to enhance the nativity scene ('cause pine trees are native to Bethlehem, right?! LOL). Next, we found stockings and stocking holders. As you can imagine, we ended up needing a second shopping cart!

When the kids saw the screen of the cash register tallying up the cost at the end of our spree, their eyes grew wide, and nervous energy emitted from their bodies. They started reaching for things that hadn't been paid for yet, offering to put them back. I thanked them for their kindness but explained that this was something I wanted to do, and I wasn't going to let something as silly as spending a lot of money take anything away from us decorating for the first Christmas in my new house.

Yes, my bank account took a significant hit that night, but the ROI I got from spending time with my kids has been incalculable. We lugged the bags and boxes through the front door and began putting everything up. Juliana made hot chocolate while Ty organized our haul into piles that made sense. I hooked up my phone to a speaker and started bumping my Christmas playlist on Spotify like we were having a house party.

Together, we got the tree set up soundly in its base, then built the other layers. When we plugged the tree lights in, we were overjoyed to see they magically worked on the first try! From there, we unpacked our ornaments and, with no strategy other than instinct, decorated our Christmas tree. We also unpacked the nativity scene and the historically inaccurate but aesthetically pleasing pine trees and arranged them on the ledge looking from the living room into the kitchen.

One of the few things I'd kept from the divorce was an electric fireplace we'd picked up from Big Lots while I was stationed at Fort Campbell, Kentucky. It was the prominent piece of furniture besides my navy blue, L-shaped sectional couch. The fireplace was dwarfed by the wall it was positioned against until we put the Christmas tree next to it. We put our stocking holders on the "mantle" of the fireplace and hung our stockings with care. Then, we ordered pizza and got to work putting our white Christmas tree up, positioning it so it would be seen from the street and sidewalk through the bay window in the kitchen. Juliana was adamant that she'd decorate the tree, so Ty and I collected the trash and flattened all the cardboard boxes so they would fit into the recycling bin.

Once the pizza arrived, we nestled up on the couch and laughed ourselves silly watching *The Santa Clause* and

Home Alone while chowing down on our meal. By the end of the night, we had each fallen asleep somewhere in the middle of a random Christmas movie we found on Netflix. Somehow, for the first time, I fell asleep on a Saturday, ignorant and blissfully unaware that tomorrow was Sunday and I wouldn't see my kids for a week.

It wasn't the house or the decorations or even the tree. It was the fact that for the first time since I'd taken off my uniform, the place I lived in finally felt like home.

What I'd Tell You If You're Isolating Right Now

If you're sitting in silence right now, wondering whether you're even worth the effort, hear me: You are absolutely worth the effort. But you have to realize you are standing at a fork in the road. The choices you make in the next few weeks and months will shape the man or woman you become.

You are not broken beyond repair. But you are hurt. You are wounded. And wounded things need healing—not shame.

The good news? It's not about changing your whole life overnight. It's about choosing to get 1 percent better every day. Fifteen minutes a day. One conversation. One workout. One prayer. One small win.

1.01 x 365 = 37 percent growth in a year.

Imagine being 37 percent better in your relationships. Your faith. Your fitness. Your purpose.

You're not weak for needing help. You're wise for reaching for it.

And brother/sister—you're still in the fight. You just need to pick the right weapon this time: connection.

Reflection and Recon

- When did isolation start feeling safer than connection?
- What lies has isolation been whispering to you?
- Who could you reach out to today—not to be "fixed" but just to be seen?

Call to Action: Choose Presence Over Withdrawal

Tonight, do one thing that requires you to be present with people—even if it's uncomfortable.

Sit with your family instead of retreating to the TV or doomscrolling on your phone. Call a friend and listen, even if you don't talk much. Go to a coffee shop or public space just to be around life happening.

You don't have to say anything profound. You don't have to open up all at once. You just have to show up.

As John Donne wrote, "No man is an island, entire of itself." We're not meant to live cut off from one another. Isolation whispers that you're safer alone, but presence is what keeps you alive, rooted, and part of the greater whole.

Every time you choose to stay present, you're choosing connection over withdrawal, life over silence.

You're still in the fight. And you're still needed—fully, imperfectly, and right here.

CHAPTER 5

FREEDOM IN CLARITY

You're not the only one. You've just been led to believe you are.

My Story: Going to the VA

I'd heard all the horror stories, how the VA doesn't care about you, how they will try to screw you out of your rating, etc. My experience with the VA couldn't have been more different. I think it was in November or December 2020 when I had the initial phone call with my VA rep, the person who would champion me through the claims process. I took the call from my truck in the driveway. It was cold out. Frost still clung to the trees, and the grass, dancing as the sunlight reflected off the frozen surface, taunted me about the winter that was coming.

My rep was a patient gentleman who sounded like he was my age. With a slight gravelly twang to his voice, suggesting an Appalachian upbringing, he was confident, compassionate, polite, and supportive. He assured me that he was on my side and he would guide me through the process.

The call must have lasted two hours. He walked and talked me through everything from the top of my head to the bottom of my feet, including explaining how my appointments would go. Due to the impact of COVID-19, the VA was slammed, and they had outsourced a lot of the scheduling of appointments. I had an online portal, and when I logged into it, I would have access to a dashboard that would show me required appointments, which I could schedule at my convenience. All in all, it was a user-friendly system, and I only ever had one hiccup throughout the dozens of appointments scheduled over the next few months.

The appointment I remember the most was my mental health appointment. As the saying goes, I was "as nervous as a long-tailed cat in a room full of rocking chairs." The mental health professional I met with was a blonde woman in her late fifties or early sixties with glasses perched halfway down her nose. Her office looked like a mental health professional starter kit—diplomas on the wall, scores of books creatively placed on the rustic cherry bookshelves, a pervasive scent of old paper and hand sanitizer.

Yeah. I'm about to get my head shrunk, I thought to myself.

To lock in the appointment, I'd already submitted documentation of "significant emotional events" from my service. As I mentioned at the beginning of the book, I'm not an operator, but I did have my fair share of excitement throughout my career. I picked the top three and described them as best I could.

As my mental health provider reviewed my paperwork, the room was so quiet I swear you could hear my heart beating. My posture was stiff, rigid, uneasy—so much so that it felt like my shoulders were hunched up to my ears, regardless of how hard I tried to ease them back down. My arms were folded across my chest, and my feet were planted on the floor, slightly more than shoulder width apart like I was getting ready to take a charge in a basketball game. If the FBI needed a photo of defensive body language for their interview handbook, I could have modeled for it.

After the mental health professional reviewed my paperwork and started talking with me, my left foot lost its anchor and began its trademark bounce. The bounce is rooted in the balls of my feet, which remain anchored to the ground, while my calf drives my heel up and down—noticeably. So much so, in fact, that I have received comments on how much I make my truck shake when we are stopped at a red light.

I don't recall the details of the conversation. I do remember going through the events in a fair amount of detail. She wasn't going to let me broad stroke everything and pretend like I was fine when I clearly was not. What I do remember is her telling me I had PTSD, anxiety, and depression. When I heard those words, I simultaneously felt like I'd gotten punched square in the breadbasket and like I was taking the most relaxing hot shower of my life.

See, when my ADHD brain analyzed that I had PTSD, anxiety, and depression, I realized two things at the same time. The first was that I was not invincible, that I was in fact not okay, that my armor had been cracked. That was the gut punch. At the same time, I realized that the mood swings, irritability, nightmares, self-isolation, etc., were the result of something, that I wasn't crazy. My problems had a name—they had been identified. That meant I could get to work on them, could defeat them. That was the hot, relaxing shower.

And what happens when you take a steaming hot shower at the end of a long day or week? Your muscles relax. Slowly. Sitting in the laughably stereotypical leather chair, I felt the tension in my shoulders slowly start to release. My hands, which had clenched into fists, unballed, and I laid my palms gently on my trousers, fingers and thumbs extended and joined at the cusp of my kneecap, just like they'd taught us to do at the promotion board. I exhaled deeply, softly, not sharply. It was liberating. I'd thought there was something wrong with me, and in theory there was, but it wasn't *me.* It wasn't my fault; it wasn't a character flaw or a personality trait. My mind and body had simply responded and adapted to the events the best way they knew how.

Admittedly, I felt shame wash over me shortly after. Why? Because, like many who grew up in the same generation, both in life and even more so in the military, we had spoken negatively about PTSD, anxiety, and depression. There was a strong stigma, a negative connotation, not only associated with those words and symptoms but with the people who had them. Funny how the paradigm shift happens when you're not on the outside looking in anymore, right?

Walking out of that appointment, I didn't feel fixed, but I did feel informed. Naming the problem didn't solve everything, but it gave me something solid to push against. And in my world, once I know my enemy, I know how to fight.

Silent Baggage

You expect the noise to stop . . . the engines, the gunfire, the radios, the shouting. And it does. But what replaces it is something quieter . . . and heavier.

I don't mean flashbacks or nightmares—at least not just those. I mean standing in a grocery store staring at forty-seven brands of peanut butter and wondering why you feel completely out of place. I mean hearing a door slam and having your heart spike because somewhere, deep down, your body still thinks it needs to protect people. I mean sitting at a family barbecue, smiling on the outside while your insides whisper, *You don't belong here.*

The hardest part about coming home isn't what people think it is. It's not finding a job, although as we discussed earlier, that can be daunting. It's not learning how to dress without the right combination of pouches for every mission. It's not trying to explain acronyms that civilians don't understand.

It's the feeling that no one sees what you're carrying. And worse . . . that maybe they don't want to.

The war didn't end when you got back home. The battlefield just changed.

Now, it shows up as anxiety at the dinner table. It shows up in your sleep. In how quickly you snap at the people you love. It shows up in the way you can't quite look at yourself in the mirror—because the person who led troops into combat now feels powerless in their own house.

I've been there.

I had spent two decades giving everything to the army. What I got in return was honorable service, yes. A legacy, maybe. But also . . . a quiet home, an identity crisis, and a divorce.

I was expected to move on.

But the truth is that veterans don't "move on." We carry on. And some days, that load is heavy as hell.

Living in Yellow

When I came home, I thought I was ready. I wasn't.

We used a red-yellow-green system downrange to measure alertness. Red was danger. Yellow was caution. Green was safety.

After my last deployment, which was not a combat deployment, I was supposed to live in green. Instead, I lived in yellow. In every store, on every street, in every quiet moment at home, I was still scanning, still calculating, still waiting for something to go wrong.

It wasn't anger or rage. It was survival mode. And it exhausted me. It exhausted the people around me too, even if they couldn't explain why. And the worst part was I didn't even realize it at first.

It had become normal.

Bringing the Battlefield Home

It showed up in little ways: Planning grocery trips like missions. Mapping my day like an operations order. Living by calendars because the unknown felt like a threat.

My family tried to understand. Some days, they did. Most days, they couldn't.

And no one really knew how heavy the guilt was. The guilt of making it back when better men didn't. The guilt of living when others didn't get the chance. The guilt of wondering if I was honoring their sacrifice—or just existing.

When Healing Finally Started

Healing didn't come all at once. It wasn't a motivational speech or a flag-waving moment. It came sitting across from a VA mental health professional who finally said what no one else had: "You're not broken. You survived some hellish experiences, and it changed you. But it didn't destroy you."

That acknowledgment cracked something open inside me. It gave me permission to stop hiding the struggle. To admit there was a wound without believing I was weak.

Healing isn't forgetting the war. Healing is refusing to let the war be the last thing that defines you. And healing—real healing—is a marathon, not a sprint. It's a battle of its own—one you have to choose to fight every single day.

Reflection and Recon

- Where are you living today: red, yellow, or green?
- What habit or instinct from deployment still clings to you, and how is it serving or hurting you now?
- How would it feel to believe healing isn't betrayal—it's honor?

Call to Action: Lower Your Guard Without Losing Yourself

Pick one environment tomorrow—just one—and consciously lower your alert status.

- Go to a store without planning every exit route.
- Sit somewhere without obsessing about who's coming through the door.
- Let your shoulders drop. Let your breathing slow. Let yourself *be here.*

You're not dishonoring anyone by standing down. You're proving that survival wasn't a fluke. You're showing that warriors don't just fight. They endure. They rebuild. They rise again.

And brother/sister, you're still rising.

CHAPTER 6

SAYING YES TO ADVENTURES

You don't need a formation to find your people.

My Story: Opening Up to Happiness

After my divorce, I was pretty much done with the idea of dating and finding someone ever again. I'm not a small talk kind of guy, and asking or being asked "What's your favorite color?" and other mindless, meaningless conversation fillers on first dates was abysmal.

All of that changed when Caitlyn and I matched online. What really sparked my interest was that she said she wanted someone who "says yes to adventures." She also recognized and appreciated a *Ted Lasso* clip on my profile in which a former player tells the owner that she shouldn't "settle for fine—you deserve someone who makes you feel like you've been struck by lightning." That's something I think everyone deserves, and the fact she knew it was from *Ted Lasso*, my favorite show, really intrigued me.

As online dating goes, we had some fun conversations over text, which led to phone conversations. This was when things got real for me. Our first call was two hours long. Sure, there was a little small talk, but we had genuine, meaningful, in-depth talks about life.

The next night, we talked for two and a half hours, and the night after that, we talked for three hours. These conversations were paramount in our relationship because we were honest and forthright with each other, and they really set the foundation for things to come.

These candid conversations led to a pivotal moment in the same week—our second date, a day trip to Chicago for a Cubs game. Caitlyn came up with the idea, and I promptly agreed, adding, "Why don't I get the Cubs tickets regardless, and we can drive together?" Caitlyn said yes, and I was ecstatic.

I also knew that since the game was in just a few days, her family was going to freak out if she went on a four-hour drive with someone she hadn't even met yet. So, I took a picture of my license plate and my driver's license to calm their nerves. (I was military police for twenty years in the army and understood that this is how serial killer documentaries start LOL.)

Our first date was the night before the Cubs game. We met at The Morrie—a fun, contemporary bar—in Royal Oak. I greeted her in the parking lot, and we walked in together. To my delight, the conversations were just as real and compelling in person as they had been on the phone.

The next day, we took off for Chicago together, and Caitlyn drove for the last little bit since it was my first time visiting the Windy City. She was smart and brought us in via Lakeshore Drive so I could see the good side of Chicago. Then, she took me around the city, showing me some cool sights, where she went to college, and where she used to live. Wrigley was a great experience, and we had a fantastic time at the game.

Things moved a little fast after that, as Memorial Day was only a week or so later, and she was hosting a party that close friends and family would be attending. I showed up before everyone arrived so I could meet her mom, Barb, and we had a wonderful conversation. The Memorial Day party went off without a hitch, and I truly enjoyed meeting so many people who were important to Caitlyn. If I recall correctly, I even worked the grill for a bit and got complimented on my grill-master skills.

The next day, Caitlyn and I flew to Orlando for our first trip together. When we arrived, we drove to Daytona Beach, a place I'd always wanted to see, so we could grab drinks at a cool beach bar and walk along the ocean before going to check into our hotel. Then, between lounging by the pool and drinking Orlando Vices—the local version of Miami Vices—we had a really cool dinner at The Hampton Social, which included the best oysters ever; saw *Top Gun: Maverick* in a 4D theater; had a great date night at a mock Italian village in Universal Studios; and went to Sea World. One of the most memorable moments was when we went on what was supposed to be a romantic Ferris wheel ride on the tallest Ferris wheel east of the

Mississippi. It's four hundred feet tall, and I hate heights, so I couldn't get out of it fast enough! All in all, Orlando was a blast, and I felt good about what was to come.

In early July, I had the opportunity to meet more of Caitlyn's family when we flew to California. Barb's husband at the time owned a seventy-foot sailboat and took us all around San Diego and even into international waters. We had a wonderful experience and lots of laughs as I tried paddleboarding.

I remember one of her friends asking if I knew what I was doing regarding my relationship with Caitlyn, and I said yes—because this was a two-way interview. I explained that I wasn't the only one under the microscope; I was intently examining Caitlyn's friends and family as well, as this would be the family I was potentially joining. Since I'd been married before, this was extremely important to me; I'd never felt like I belonged in my ex's family, even though they'd known me since high school for a cumulative seventeen years. I was determined to ensure the family my kids and I joined liked me and wanted me to be a part of them as opposed to just tolerating me. All signs indicated that things were going to go very well.

The next milestone came in late July when I introduced Caitlyn to my kids. This was a huge step and not just for obvious reasons. See, I had told myself I wouldn't introduce anyone to the kids until we had been together for at least six months. Yet here I was, just two months in, introducing them. Things went well, and then it was Caitlyn's turn to get put to the test.

The first week of August, my son had a weeklong baseball tournament in Myrtle Beach, and my mom and stepdad were coming to cheer him on. This meant Caitlyn was going to have to deal with me, the South Carolina heat in the peak of summer, long hours at a baseball field, and potential future in-laws for several consecutive days. Fortunately, I can confidently say she passed with flying colors, and we had a great time.

The rest of the summer was fairly uneventful—lots of dates, getting to know the kids, and work. For Labor Day, Caitlyn, Ty, Juliana, and I went to Missouri, where she got to meet my two closest friends and their families. They all loved Caitlyn and were genuinely happy that we'd found each other. This was significantly important to me, as I had known my friends since 2002, and we had deployed with each other. Their opinions mattered.

That being said, Caitlyn and I continued to have important discussions about what we wanted out of life and what our future(s) looked like. Earlier in the summer, I had volunteered to coach the high school's fall baseball team, and I found out in August that I had been selected. This was when I really saw a future together forever with Caitlyn because she not only encouraged me to coach, but she was wildly supportive of my all-in enthusiasm. She saw how much it meant to me, how much I loved being around the boys and making a positive impact on their lives. She showed up to the games, whether they were in the morning and in the cold or in the afternoon when it was still warm enough to need sunscreen. She even helped me find a way to host an end-of-season banquet for the team.

Unbeknownst to her, around this time, I knew I wanted to marry her. I had talked to the kids about it, and they were all in. My friends had seen in person how happy we were together, so they were all for it as well. So I connected with Caitlyn's closest friends and began planning the proposal.

In late October, I finally had everything prepared, and I sent out a PowerPoint presentation that was the equivalent of an actual mission in combat: a scavenger hunt of dates we had gone on in Michigan. Each point in the scavenger hunt had a letter on the back, which eventually spelled out *This Is Us*, our favorite TV show. She made my wildest dreams come true when she said yes on that day, December 22.

For most, that would be the end of the story, but not for us.

In early November, I got a wild hair and applied for an opening as an assistant baseball coach at Hillsdale College. At the time, I didn't think I had a chance, but I didn't want to live with the regret of not trying. Caitlyn had been entirely supportive of me during the process, but there was a really big stipulation, which, quite frankly, made us both nervous. I would be hired as an assistant coach on a stipend—so full-time work for part-time pay. With Caitlyn's encouragement, I accepted the job and got to live my dream of being a baseball coach. She looked past the fear of me taking a significant pay cut, the long hours, and the unknown of what a coach's life/time away was really like and "let" me pursue this avenue, and for that, I am eternally grateful.

Two days before we got married, on October 4, 2023, Caitlyn and I hosted friends and family at our house. I made chicken adobo and carne asada on the grill right next to corn and flour tortillas, so they were warm and fresh when people made their plates. We covered the island in the kitchen with tin foil and put out various tortilla chips, a bowl of homemade Mexican rice, and all the taco toppings. Of course, Caitlyn made her famous margaritas.

Everyone who would be in town before the rehearsal dinner was at the house—a solid fifty-plus people—except two. One of my dearest friends (and one of the funniest people on the planet), Justin, and his wife, April. He texted that they had landed, but it was taking them unusually long to get to my house from the airport, which was only a fifteen-to-twenty-minute drive. They hadn't been able to come to Missouri the year before, and I hadn't seen them in four years. Needless to say, I was extremely eager to see them again.

After the food was cooked, I literally stood in my driveway, pacing back and forth, waiting for their arrival. Once I saw the turn signal illuminate on an obvious rental car, my heart skipped a beat. Justin threw the car into park, jumped out, and embraced me in a bear hug, the kind that puts all the broken pieces of you back together, even if only for a moment.

Caitlyn had been watching me, saw everything go down, and she scampered down the front porch to introduce herself to April, with whom she became instant friends. Caitlyn could tell there was something special about Justin and April and acknowledged the joy and calm that had overcome me when they arrived.

Unintentionally, Justin and I pretty much ignored everyone the rest of the night as we broke into the secret, comically large bottle of Bulleit Bourbon Caitlyn had picked up from Costco and thought she'd been able to hide from me. I felt a slight tinge of guilt (but not much) as Justin and I put in work on that bottle, catching up, telling jokes and lies, laughing until the wee hours of the morning. In a drunken stupor the next day, we were a bit embarrassed when we realized we'd killed more than half of the bottle. Oh well—weddings are parties; we just got it going a little sooner than expected.

On Thursday, October 5, I spent the morning making airport runs and loading up vehicles with stuff for the wedding. My dad hosted the rehearsal dinner at Slows Bar BQ in downtown Detroit. Caitlyn and the bridal party did a wonderful job with signage and décor, and every seat in the joint was packed. Caitlyn wore a white cocktail dress under a jean jacket bedazzled with "Wifey" in cursive across the back. She looked absolutely gorgeous.

After we ate, we presented our bridal party with gifts. Caitlyn got her bridesmaids a tote bag with a wallet, their wedding jewelry, and stuff like that. For the groomsmen, I got the belt and tie they would wear and an insulated Yeti-type tumbler with their favorite NFL team on it. Caitlyn teases me about this because she kinda just called each bridesmaid up and handed them their stuff, whereas I gave a mini speech about each groomsman and their impact on my life before handing them their gifts.

All in all, it was a great rehearsal dinner, and we all went to our separate corners for the night. We stayed at the Westin in downtown Detroit, which was only a ten-minute drive from the venue, The Roostertail. My son stayed in the room with me. Caitlyn, my daughter, and her bridesmaids had a suite so they could get ready the next morning.

On the morning of the wedding, on October 6, Ty went with me as I got my beard trimmed and cleaned up. I grabbed him some McDonald's on the way back to the hotel, but I couldn't think about eating. I'd been up since 2 a.m., and I was wired. It was the same feeling you get when you roll outside the wire on your first mission downrange—some nerves, a lot of excitement.

Caitlyn and I did the first look on a gorgeous, black-and-white marble stairwell and landing. When I felt her hand land softly on my shoulder, signaling it was okay to turn around and look, my heart leapt. I turned slowly, taking time to appreciate the moment. Spotlit from the sun shining through windows above and behind her was my bride-to-be in a stunning, deep-plunge, fit-and-flare, lace wedding dress with sleeves made from the train. My eyes burned for the first time in years as tears of joy filled them. I could barely catch my breath. I think I managed to squeak out, "You look incredible, babe."

We boarded our limousine and headed to Parker's Alley for the first round of photos. It was a perfect blend of the industrial heartbeat that Detroit has embodied, combined with the modern, contemporary vibes of a city in the midst of a renaissance.

From there, we went to Belle Isle. We'd been told the historic and iconic water fountain would be shut off that time of year, but when the bus pulled up, we were pleasantly surprised to see the water flowing beautifully, with mist being created by a rather stiff but fairly cooperative breeze. We moved to the shore of the Detroit River, where we captured some incredible photos with the Motor City skyline behind us. Then it was showtime. We were en route to The Roostertail.

Our event coordinator, Nicole, was worth every penny. She was locked in, ensuring everything had been set up according to our (Caitlyn's) specifications. As we walked to the venue, I noticed a small cake next to our wedding cake. As I got closer, I realized Caitlyn had a mini-Captain America cake made just for me. Caitlyn and the girls went to the bride's room to get ready; I went downstairs with the groomsmen to welcome guests.

We got married on a wooden landing attached to The Roostertail. Right on the water, which both of us love. The tricky part was getting there; the only way on or off the landing was a three-hundred-plus-foot walk down the dock. With gorgeous views of Belle Isle and Windsor in the background, we were centered under a peaked archway, which was adorned with yellow, white, and red flower bundles.

Caitlyn elected to walk herself down the aisle, but we had a special surprise. I left my spot next to my groomsmen, who, like me, were all wearing navy blue suits with cream-colored shirts, burgundy ties, and brown belts with brown shoes. I met Caitlyn where the dock and landing joined, and we walked arm in arm to the altar. The service was quick; we had a short but memorable unity ceremony toward the end.

Because Caitlyn was joining not only me but Ty and Juliana as well, she wanted to symbolize the blending of two families. She'd contacted a glass blower who had us each select a color. I picked blue; Ty, green; Caitlyn, burgundy; and Juliana, pink. We poured our colors into a bowl, which we later mailed off to be turned into a Christmas ornament, an "on the rocks" glass, a wine glass, and a paperweight.

We had a social hour after the wedding so the guests could mingle and grab some snacks while we took more pictures. The very best picture was the last one we took. A storm was approaching, and on the east side of the venue, the photographer captured a dramatic and beautiful picture of Caitlyn and me together and the city of Detroit behind us with thick clouds rolling in. We got a little rain that night but not much.

When the reception began, the wedding party entered to T.I.'s "Bring Em Out." They played their parts well and got the guests hyped up. Caitlyn and I followed it up by entering to Bruno Mars' "24K Magic." The message was clear—this was a celebration. I half C-walked, half power-skipped, dragging Caitlyn with me and spilling my drink on my sleeve, as I couldn't wait to get the party going.

The maid of honor and best man delivered their speeches but were overshadowed by Juliana giving a toast for the ages. She hates public speaking, but like her old man, she's got a way with words, and boy, did she deliver. Her voice shook at first, but she steadied and found herself. At the end, there was not a dry eye in the room.

Dinner was great, and we mingled before our first dance. We had taken this seriously and had taken dance lessons for weeks before the wedding, which was ambitious because Caitlyn had torn her ACL in March, just six months prior. On cue, as the first beat of George Strait's "I Cross My Heart" sounded, we were perfectly in sync. We spun, turned, and glided across the dance floor with precision that would make Russian ballerinas jealous until we ended with our signature move: a modern twist on the bridal dip (to avoid putting unnecessary strain on Caitlyn's knee).

The rest of the night was a blur of conversation, pictures, laughing, and dancing. It culminated with the trendy-at-the-time tradition of Taylor Swift's "Love Story." I'd never done it, but perfectly on time, I dropped to one knee in a mock proposal to Caitlyn with all our friends around us dancing and jumping while shout-singing the lyrics when Romeo asks Juliet to marry him.

It was a hell of a wedding. People still talk about it to this day.

Rebuilding Your Team

When I left the army, I thought I was prepared to be alone. After all, I'd been in combat. I'd slept on the ground. I'd gone weeks with minimal communication from home. Solitude didn't scare me.

But what I didn't expect—what hit harder than I care to admit—was the absence of my people.

No more early morning jokes during PT. No more shoulder-to-shoulder grind on the range. No more world-class insults and trash talk in the motor pool. No more looking across the room and knowing without a word that someone has your back.

The uniform gave me a team by default.

But post-service? You've got to build your team—on purpose. And that's where a lot of us get stuck. We don't trust easily. We don't want to ask for help. We don't want to be disappointed by people who haven't walked through what we have.

But here's what I've come to believe: Isolation might feel safe, but it's a slow death for the soul.

You were built for connection. The same way you once fought with a team—you're meant to heal with one too.

Rebuilding your team doesn't mean replacing your old brothers and sisters. It means surrounding yourself with people who want to walk with you now—with the version of you that's figuring life out without camouflage and boots.

You're not alone in this chapter either. Let's talk about what it looks like to build your circle again—intentionally, authentically, and without apology.

From Chain of Command to Circle of Trust

When I got out of the military, the silence crept in slowly. At first, I didn't notice.

I had my "core four"—my closest brothers. Guys who'd show up if I called, no matter what. But about a month after retirement, the texts slowed. The phone stopped buzzing.

Then my last CSM texted me—out of the blue. And it hit me: I missed the brotherhood more than I ever thought I would. But that moment also reminded me just how high the caliber of the people I had served with was.

My CSM wasn't just a leader—he was one of the men who changed my life. On our last deployment, I told him I planned to go into law enforcement. He looked me in the eye and said, "Why do you want to be a cop? You have so much more to offer the world than continuing to put your life on the line."

I didn't fully understand it then. But I heard him. And now, here I am—coaching, writing, leading, and building something bigger than myself.

Staying Connected to the Old Team

I still keep in touch with the guys. Honestly, it's one of the few reasons I even have social media. I send out daily motivational videos. We trade memes, GIFs, reels. We comment on each other's wins and milestones.

Just a few weeks ago, a buddy I was stationed with in Germany FaceTimed me—with another buddy from the same unit on the screen. We had all played softball together over there, and they had linked up playing softball in Texas. I was so thrilled that they thought of me and took the time to FaceTime me.

It was like no time had passed.

Two years ago, three soldiers I led at Fort Campbell called me together—just to talk to "Dad." And that's what I'll always be to them. Not because of rank. But because of how much we loved each other.

My Story: My Top Teammate

If you can't tell, music is a very big part of my life. I have a playlist for everything. The gym? Check. Cleaning the house? Check. Taking a shower? Check. Songs often have the words and evoke the emotions we can't articulate ourselves. Dustin Lynch's "Cowboys and Angels" perfectly encapsulates the dynamic that is me and Caitlyn. I'm more rugged, raw, and rough around the edges. Caitlyn is refined and elegant.

I've lived in a lot of places, seen a lot of things, and met people from all walks of life, religions, and socioeconomic backgrounds. But I've never encountered anyone like Caitlyn. She is the kindest, sweetest person I have ever met. She's innocent in that she sees life in a way most of us don't. She loves animals—to the point she threw a mini temper tantrum about going to Sea World with me when we first started dating. She has an app on her phone called "Be My Eyes" that connects her to a stranger in an airport, grocery store, or other public area who is blind or hard of sight, and she can literally be their eyes and help them navigate their environment. Who does that?! Caitlyn does.

She is the best friend anyone could ask for. She is constantly thinking about others, looking for some way, any way, to celebrate them. She is also a master event planner. You remember the story about me and the kids decorating the Christmas tree? Yeah, that style didn't last long after she moved in LOL. We now have soft white lights on our tree and a very Ralph Lauren vibe when we decorate. Neither the kids nor I care, and we love how classy our house looks this time of year.

To continue with the song lyrics theme, the start of the second verse of Post Malone's song with Blake Shelton, "Pour Me a Drink," says, "Bourbon brown eyes tryna get me drunk." That describes Caitlyn's eyes perfectly—they are intoxicating. Warm and inviting with a soft glow when she's happy and things are going well. They dim, almost as if being shielded, when she is sad, and intriguingly, they sparkle when she's about to cry. They are the most comforting things I have ever seen. When I look into her eyes, all my worries fade away.

The most important decision you will ever make is who you choose to be your spouse. Well, I chose wisely. Caitlyn is a hell of a businesswoman and a natural conversationalist, and she loves to see people succeed. She has been a rock, a sounding board, and my biggest cheerleader during this endeavor. As I have wound through different career paths and ultimately embraced this role as an author, podcaster, speaker, and small business owner, she has shone like a desert sunrise. She has been there every step of the way, encouraging me, challenging me, sharing my endeavors, and believing in me.

I think what makes us a great couple is that we are interdependent of each other. What that means is we are two independent people who could and would be just fine on their own. However, together, we are even better. We enhance each other through mutual support and love for one another. As two independent people, we are strong individually and unbreakable together.

I once prayed to God to not waste the painful stuff, and he didn't. He sent me my very own angel to guide me on this journey.

Finding My New Team

My wife, kids, core four, and family were already cemented as teammates.

Then there's my former head coach at Hillsdale. We still catch up often, and every conversation reminds me how much I learned from him. Even though I didn't leave in the most professional way (more on this later), he's never shown anything but respect—and that means the world to me.

My pastor and life coach? He's been transformative. He gave me the clarity and the courage to finally write this book.

But most important of all: Jesus. I surrendered my heart, and that relationship changed everything. He's not just part of the team—He's the foundation of it.

What I Look for Now in a Teammate

If you're in my inner circle now, you've earned it. I look for:

- Authenticity.
- Integrity.
- Empathy.
- Drive.
- People who challenge me without disrespecting me.
- People who walk in honesty, not perfection.

I'm even working on a book about this exact idea—because building the right team in your next chapter might be the difference between growth and implosion.

What I'd Say to the Veteran Who Doesn't Trust Anyone Anymore

I understand that feeling. But I'm going to challenge you with something hard: That mistrust? It might not be about them. It might be about you.

You've listened to the lies. You've isolated yourself. You've allowed bitterness or fear to build walls around your heart.

But here's the truth: Trust and respect don't have to be earned first. They have to be lost.

Don't go through life expecting the worst in people. Start expecting the best.

That doesn't mean handing your heart to everyone. You can be honest with everyone without being vulnerable with everyone.

Honesty is for all. Transparency is for a few. Build your squad accordingly. And don't rob the right people of the chance to be there for you just because the wrong ones weren't.

Reflection and Recon

- Who's in your squad now—and who shouldn't be?
- Are you expecting the best in people—or preparing for the worst?
- What kind of teammate are you right now?

Call to Action: Draft Your [Fire] Team

Travis Kelce once told the story of a turning point in his life—a day in college when his coach pulled him aside and said, "Travis, you're draining me."

It wasn't about the people around him—it was about him. Kelce realized he wasn't adding energy, encouragement, or inspiration. He was pulling from others without giving back.

That's when he learned the fountains and drains parable:

> Fountains pour into others—they inspire, encourage, and make the people around them better.
>
> Drains pull from others—taking time, energy, and joy without replenishing them.

Kelce made a conscious decision to stop being a drain. He worked on showing up with positivity, gratitude, and value. Over time, he transformed into a fountain—not just in football but in life. That shift helped shape the leader and teammate he is today. Even his fiancée, Taylor Swift, mentioned it on the Kelce brothers' podcast—how she sees and appreciates the way he brings energy and positivity into every room.

Now it's your turn. Take a hard look at your circle—and yourself.

1. Start with you.
    - Are you a fountain or a drain?

   - Do people leave conversations with you feeling encouraged, energized, and valued—or worn down and discouraged?

2. Look outward.
   - Who in your life is a true fountain—pouring into you, lifting you up, and making you better?
   - Who are the drains—those who consistently take without giving, pull you into negativity, or sap your motivation?
3. Make a choice.
   - Limit the influence of drains.
   - Invest more time and energy into your fountains.
   - And most importantly, become the kind of fountain you want around you.

Take one step today:

- Offer genuine encouragement to someone who needs it.
- Express gratitude to someone who's poured into you.
- Bring a solution instead of just pointing out a problem.

Your best energy is a gift—don't waste it on those who drain you.

Build a circle that makes you better . . . and be the reason they get better too.

CHAPTER 7

NO ONE CARES HOW MUCH YOU KNOW UNTIL THEY KNOW HOW MUCH YOU CARE

"A good coach can change a game. A great coach can change a life." —John Wooden

My Story: What a True Leader Looks Like

Growing up, I played all the typical sports kids in the eighties and nineties played. I *loved* competing, especially because I was small. Getting to compete allowed me to access something primal in me, where I was required to be tough, resilient, competent, confident, and a good teammate. I was a pretty decent baseball and football player. In fact, I was scouted by the Phillies and Indians in high school and could have played D2 or D3 football had I not torn my ACL my junior year.

Once I became a father, I knew if the opportunity presented itself, I would coach my son. While I was stationed in Germany, I got the chance with basketball, flag football, and baseball.

The first time I knew I made a positive impact as a coach came during the last basketball game of the season. For context, the kids were young—in second and third grade. We played half court on portable basketball hoops set at seven or eight feet.

A little girl on the team had not scored a point all season, but she was a delight to be around, always full of good energy, hustling, and trying her best. There was less than a minute left of the last game of the season, and she still hadn't scored a point. The kids kept track of their own stats and knew, instinctively, to get her the ball. Suddenly, everything fell into place. My son got the inbound pass, took it downcourt, and faked a pass to the best player on our team, who was being double-teamed. He passed it to the little girl, who was wide open. She caught it, set her feet, and made her shot. It was like something out of a Hallmark movie. I swear time slowed down. I remember the ball hitting the top right corner of the square and falling through the net. Textbook Tim Duncan shot.

I couldn't contain myself. I ran down the court, jumped in the air, and pumped my fist like I'd won a national championship. In my mind, I looked like Michael Jordan after hitting his game-winning shot over Cleveland in the 1989 playoffs. I'm certain I was not as graceful or athletic, but watching her make that bucket and score her first points carried as much emotional weight in my life as hitting that game winner did for MJ. She ran over and gave me a hug, and our whole team celebrated.

Years later, my now ex-wife put together a book full of letters from people I had served with for my retirement party. Apparently, my ex was still friends with the girl's mom on Facebook, and when she posted about building the book, six years after I had coached her daughter in basketball for only one season, the mom wrote a letter. She thanked me for coaching her daughter, for believing in her, and for celebrating her. I was blown away.

I coached my son on and off at different bases and ages, from T-ball to Little League, through the awkward middle school travel ball era. I got my first head coaching gig in 2019 for the county baseball league but had to leave halfway through the season because I was deployed.

In the fall of 2021, I was working at the Michigan Senate, and my son was a freshman in high school. His school had a fall baseball league, and I saw there was an opening for an assistant coach. I applied and was overjoyed to earn the opportunity. It was a blast but very different compared to coaching my son at the previous levels. I learned a lot that season and hoped to have the chance to coach again.

In the spring of 2022, I was not an assistant coach, but I was one of the dads who helped keep score for my son's freshman baseball team. Then, that fall, I got the privilege of being the head coach for the team. Caitlyn, who I was dating at that time, came to all the games and saw that

I had a real passion for it. I even held an end-of-season banquet with awards, personal recognition for each player, and what I hope was a memorable speech.

Shortly after, I saw an opening for an assistant baseball coach at Hillsdale College, and I eagerly applied. On Veterans Day 2022, the head coach, a man named Tom, gave me a call. It was more of a vibe check than anything. He liked what I had to say, felt we would get along, and invited me for an in-person interview. The interview went really well, and a couple of weeks later, I was invited back to meet with Tom and the associate head coach, Ryan. We walked the campus, checked out the facilities, and went out to lunch to get to know each other on a more personal level.

A few weeks later, I was back for my final interview, which was with the vice president of Hillsdale College. I met with Tom prior, and he pumped me up and said I was going to kill it. I believed him, but for the first time ever going into an interview, I was nervous. I wanted this job so badly. The interview was fine, but I definitely stumbled on stuff I had prepared for.

At one point, the VP asked me, "Who do you think has more impact on a player—a coach or a professor?" I wanted to blurt out "coach," but I didn't know how to quantify it. A pregnant pause filled the room. After probably five or six seconds but what felt like an eternity, I answered, "A coach, but I don't know how to justify it." See, Hillsdale is a highly intellectual, academically challenging school, and I didn't want to come off as someone who thought that sports were more valuable than education.

But the VP agreed, calming my nerves. He said, "Kevin, the passion you have for the game and the students is obvious. The answer to this question is simple. It's math. As a coach, you will get three hours a day, five days a week with the kids before the season starts, and so many more hours once it does start and you're traveling. You have exponentially more time and influence with the student athletes, so it's imperative that we pick the right people."

I was blown away. That was an incredible answer and way to describe the impact a coach, especially at the college level, has on their players. The walk from the VP's office back to the baseball office was long and somber. I thought for sure I had blown it. When I sulked through the doorway, Tom asked me how it went. I just looked at him sheepishly, like a dog who just got caught peeing on the rug.

"That bad, huh?" Ryan said from his desk behind me.

"I dunno," I replied morosely.

Turning back to Tom, I noticed he had one of the coach's practice hats in his hand. "Couldn't have been that bad," he grinned. "Welcome to Hillsdale."

I left my job at the Michigan Senate and started my new journey as a college baseball coach on January 9, 2023. Tom ordered dozens of pizzas and introduced me to the team as we watched the NCAA Football National

Championship. I met every single player and was beyond impressed with how professional, smart, curious, and fun they were.

For the next seven months, I drove eighty-five miles one way, an hour and a half commute from Plymouth to Hillsdale College. And I had the time of my life—practicing on the frozen football field during January and February; going on our first trip to Lee University where we upset a pre-season nationally ranked team in a three-game series, which included what would become the third most exciting game in D2 baseball; clinching a walk-off win in the first round of the Great Midwestern Athletic Conference championship at Prasco Field. Coaching college baseball has been the most rewarding thing I have ever done.

Tom and Ryan are consummate professionals who demand excellence from their players. The other coach, Mike, who worked with outfielders, was beloved by all the players; he led with quiet confidence and patience, and when he spoke, *everyone* listened. I was the catching coach, which was pretty easy because my two upperclassman catchers, Jaekob and Sean, were amazing and needed very little coaching. My freshman catcher, John, was a sponge and loved to work and learn. Every player on that team accepted me and probably poured into me and taught me more than I did them.

The mornings were usually admin-related, and Ryan would have a player meet in "the barn," where our batting cages were. I would normally follow and try to absorb as much as I could from one of the most prolific offensive minds in college baseball. Once spring came in April, my mornings were spent on our field. I would drag it, water it, and get it prepped for practice. There is nothing like the scent of freshly cut grass, and I would get "high" from that smell as I had Luke Combs or nineties country blaring on our portable speaker.

In 2023, we had a great run and walked it off against Findlay University in the first round of the GMAC conference tournament. We got double-dipped and were eliminated two games later. I can still see the tears streaming down the players' faces, their eyes swollen and red, especially the seniors, who would never play again. It was a bittersweet moment, one I was glad to share with them because the hugs and words that followed were honest and true.

Shortly after, recruiting season started. We traveled through the Midwest, going to games starting at 7 a.m. until the last game ended around midnight, trying to find athletes who could not only compete at our level but who had the academic acumen to attend a school as difficult as Hillsdale. The coolest thing that came from my short tenure coaching at Hillsdale was the relationship I built with our left fielder, Joe. I met him in his junior year and was informed that he was commissioning into the United States Marine Corps. After Joe graduated, he held his commissioning ceremony and asked me to be his first salute.

I was humbled and honored to accept, and the ceremony was incredible. Joe's family and the team showed up to support him. As is tradition, he presented me with a silver dollar, which I got a special presentation box for. The coin, along with a picture of me, Joe, Tom, and Ryan, is proudly displayed on my desk.

When Joe completed the Basic School for Marine Corps Officers at Quantico, I had the privilege of attending his graduation. There is nothing more professional or impressive than a military ceremony, and Joe's graduation was no exception.

This perfectly encapsulated why I loved coaching. The opportunity to make a lasting impact? There's nothing better. And that's what leadership is all about.

Truth Is the Real Credential

We spend so much of our lives trying to prove that we're capable. That we know what we're doing. That we've earned the right to lead.

And in the military, that works. You get promoted by demonstrating competence. You build credibility through performance. People listen to you because your rank says they should.

But out here, in the real world? Rank doesn't matter. Résumés only go so far. And most people don't care about what you've done . . . until they know how much you actually care.

It took me a while to learn that.

I used to lead with knowledge. Experience. Authority. I thought that was enough. But the teams that grew the most—the relationships that actually worked—were the ones where I stopped trying to impress and started trying to understand.

Because at the end of the day, people don't follow you because you're the smartest person in the room. They follow you because you see them. Because they feel safe around you. Because you treat them like they matter.

That's when trust is built. That's when teams start to perform. That's when people start to open up, take ownership, and give you their best—not because they have to but because they want to.

You don't have to have all the answers. You just have to care. Not in theory. Not in your head. Out loud.

This chapter is about learning how to lead with empathy—not weakness. How to build trust the right way.

And how to live out the simple truth that's shaped every good leader I've ever known: No one cares how much you know . . . until they know how much you care.

I Wasn't the Best Coach on the Field—But I Was Present

I first embodied this truth—not in combat, not in the classroom, but on a baseball field. It was when I was coaching at Hillsdale College, and if I'm being honest? I had no business coaching college baseball. From a technical and knowledge standpoint, I was out of my depth. But

I didn't walk in pretending to be something I wasn't. I didn't show up trying to impress anybody. I showed up to serve. To help those young men become the best versions of themselves—on and off the field. And that mindset earned their respect.

I did small things. Personal things. Intentional things.

- I taught box breathing techniques to two of our players before they went to a pro workout.
- I gave graduating seniors Admiral William H. McRaven's book *Make Your Bed*.
- I put "No one cares how much you know until they know how much you care" on the chalkboard in my high school classroom.

That wasn't just a motto. It was how I led. And it changed everything.

The Definition of a Good Coach

I had a couple of good coaches growing up but never one who really brought the best out of me. It wasn't until I was in the military that I experienced authentic leadership and coaching. Noncommissioned officers (NCOs) in the military are essentially coaches and teachers. The army's definition of leadership is "to provide purpose, direction, and motivation." In line with that definition, NCOs care about you as a soldier and as a human being.

As a lifelong fan and participant in sports, I eventually realized why the role of a coach seemed to align so naturally to me. NCOs and head coaches live in the same space. Both exist between vision and execution. They translate intent into action. They take abstract goals and turn them into daily discipline, habits, and accountability.

In the military, my identity was clear. I was an NCO. I knew my role. I knew my purpose. I was responsible for standards, preparation, and people. I didn't need to be the architect of the mission to feel valuable. My value came from developing others, correcting mistakes early, and making sure the team was ready when it mattered most.

A good NCO, like a good coach, understands timing and tone: *Praise in public. Reprimand in private. Confidence is built, not crushed. Accountability is firm, but it's never humiliating.* That balance creates trust and buy-in, and it keeps people willing to give discretionary effort when it's needed most.

When you get out, that role doesn't disappear, but the environment, the ecosystem around it, does.

Many veterans struggle in transition because the leadership they carried for years no longer has a visible lane. We were coaches without a team, leaders without a locker room, responsible adults suddenly told to "figure it out" on our own. The skills were still there, but the context was gone. Without context, identity erodes. Without identity, purpose feels distant.

The best coaches and the best NCOs also understand that leadership is relational, not positional. Respect is earned through consistency, competence, and care for the people under their charge. They know their players and soldiers as individuals. They know who needs encouragement, who needs accountability, and who needs both at the same time. They build trust long before the moment it's tested.

Perhaps most importantly, neither role is about personal glory. When things go well, the team gets the credit. When things go poorly, the responsibility lands squarely on their shoulders. That quiet ownership is what separates true leaders from title holders. In both locker rooms and motor pools, leadership is less about what you say and more about what you tolerate, what you model, and what you demand every day.

Reclaiming purpose after service often starts with reframing who you have always been—not just a soldier but a developer of people. Not just a veteran but a leader who understands that performance is built long before the moment of pressure. When veterans recognize that they are still coaches in a new arena, getting out becomes less about loss and more about translation.

My first real coaching experience came when I coached our unit softball team in Germany. We won the league and the on-base tournament, which meant we got to compete against all the other European base champs at Ramstein Air Base. We took third place, and it was one of the coolest experiences.

The Moment That Changed My Leadership Forever

But truthfully, that wasn't the moment that changed the way I led. That moment came at my going-away party in Hawaii.

I had a permanent change of station to Fort Campbell, and a bunch of us squad leaders were trading questions with our first sergeant.

Then someone asked the question: "Who's the best squad leader in the company?" Most of the guys figured it'd be me. I had been the tactical command center squad leader—trusted with the commander's battlefield circulation, the commander's security, and more. I was ready to hear it.

But the first sergeant looked around the circle and said, "Kidder's not even in the top five."

What?! Why?

"He's too abrasive. He doesn't know how to talk to people."

Talk about a wake-up call. But I didn't argue.

I changed. Right then.

I made a conscious decision to adapt my leadership style—because I realized that how I carried the message mattered more than the message itself. And I've never looked back.

Empathy Isn't Weak—It's a Weapon

I've messed up plenty since then—more times than I can count. I've tried too hard to prove myself. To sound smart.

To lead with my knowledge instead of my presence. But I've learned.

Now? Empathy is the cornerstone of how I lead. I'm not perfect. But I work hard to read the room. To listen first. To see the world through other people's eyes—not just my own.

That's emotional intelligence. And it's a skill. It's not about being soft. It's about being tuned in.

What I'd Say to the Authority-Driven Veteran Who Feels Disconnected

If you're out here in the civilian world trying to lead the way you did in the military—with positional authority and "I said so" energy—and it's not landing? Let me offer this:

Zoom out.

When we focus on "I" or "me," our lens is narrow. We assume we know. We assume people should listen.

But leadership after the military isn't about command. It's about connection.

One of the best pieces of advice I've ever heard comes from *Ted Lasso*: "Be curious, not judgmental." Ask more questions. Talk less. Listen more.

You'd be amazed at how many people are just dying to be seen and heard—just like you are. It'll feel awkward at first. There will be silences. It won't feel natural. But if you can master asking questions and actually caring about the answers, you'll never have to "lead" the old way again.

People will follow you because they trust you. Because they feel safe with you. Because they believe you care.

And that's worth more than any rank you've ever worn.

The Edge That Can't Be Matched

If you led in the military, you were getting a masterclass in leadership under fire.

- High stress.
- Low resources.
- Real consequences.

You learned to make decisions fast. You learned to communicate clearly. You learned that standards matter more than rules.

Rules can be bent. But standards? They define how we do everything.

You praise in public. You reprimand in private. You empower others. You lead from the front. And when that mindset enters a family or a business? Everything gets better.

Even raising kids changes when you lead like this. If they can operate an iPad, they can do any chore in the house.

My Story: Lessons Learned, Lessons Shared

In the summer of 2023, my stepdad got throat cancer, which really shook me up. I tried to pretend like everything was fine and to be strong for my mom, but inside, I was a wreck. I had a hard time seeing the positive things in life. For the first time, I looked at being a college baseball coach as a job. I was so selfish—it's embarrassing to share. Hindsight being 20/20, I can see now there was behavioral pattern I displayed: shutting myself off and pushing others away when life got super stressful. And push people away is what I did. I was not a good teammate to Tom and Ryan and abruptly resigned.

Luckily, I wasn't abrasive about it—just very matter of fact. Even more lucky is the fact that Tom and Ryan are incredible men and leaders in their own right, and they did not hold a grudge against me. They even came to my wedding, which was only two months after I walked away. They also came to visit and watch me when I coached at the high school level the following spring. We still stay in touch; they wrote letters of recommendation for me when I moved to Arizona for a job that didn't pan out when I was trying to get back in the coaching circuit. I am forever grateful for their professionalism and even more grateful for their friendship.

After leaving Hillsdale, it took me a while to find my footing, but I ended up becoming a ninth- and eleventh-grade English teacher, as well as the varsity baseball head coach, at St. Frances Cabrini High School in Allen Park in November 2023. I had no idea what I was doing as a teacher, but I knew the teachers I had loved, respected, and loathed when I was growing up and did my best to embody their best qualities. I truly loved teaching and learning from my students. I always used the first minutes of class to try to motivate and inspire them.

On the last day of school, I gave each of my students a golf ball with my name and their class and year printed on it. This came from a lesson I used one morning, which stemmed from a famous YouTube and social media reel where a teacher uses a jar to depict life and adds golf balls, rocks, and sand to show the elements that fill our lives. As the symbolism behind each component was explained, they gained a deeper understanding of what truly matters in life. I hope they still have those and look at them from time to time to remember that message I shared with them.

In January 2024, I was finally allowed to start sports-related activities. Our indoor training facility was a small portion of the attic of the annex, which had been outfitted with netting, tees, and a pitching machine. I would arrive at 6:30 a.m. and work with anyone who wanted to hit before tryouts, which were held in March. I selected fifteen players, and we went .500 on the season, which was a huge improvement from the previous season, but I never cared about wins or losses. Baseball is the best metaphor for life that sports offers. You can do everything right in an at bat, hit a ball perfect-perfect, but a defender can make an incredible play, and you're out. Conversely, you can have a horrible at bat, stick your butt out, throw the bat at the ball, and bloop it over an infielder's head . . . and get a hit.

I did my best to build a culture of discipline and routine, to encourage my players to trust the process over results, to establish a "we before me" mentality, and to teach to be where your feet are. We hit a long losing streak cultivated by near misses, games we should have won, and although it hurt, it was a growing pain that allowed us to reach districts for the first time in over five years. The team has since gone on to win districts and put the league on notice. I was so happy to be invited into this hardworking, close-knit community and am so grateful for the opportunity. I still talk to my athletic director, many of my players have friended me on social media, and I was asked to write a recommendation letter for one of my players, who was participating in a leadership peer retreat.

In the summer of 2024, I was the head coach for the Michigan Monarchs of the Great Lakes Summer Collegiate League. If you're completely unfamiliar, during the summer, college baseball players are invited to play in a summer league to hone their skills. It's a phenomenal opportunity and one of the purest forms of baseball. They live with each other and travel all over the region to compete. My team, the Monarchs, had some serious talent and even more personality. I would drive our fifteen-passenger van and listen to the boys play Mafia, a spiced-up version of the game Werewolf. The stories and antics were epic. The baseball was tier one. My nonexistent abs would hurt from laughing so much.

I was nervous to be coaching college players again, but I realized there was no pressure. I met the players three days before our first game, handed out uniforms, ensured we got everyone's number, and held a quick get-to-know-you meeting. On our trip down to Ohio for our first game of the season, I realized they didn't need me to coach them, per se; they needed me to believe in them and give them the opportunity to get reps in and develop in the areas their real college coaches desired.

When we got to the dugout, I hung up the large version of our lineup card, and it was empty. I told the boys that I didn't know them and I didn't have video on them, so it was up to them, as a team, to determine who would play where and where they would be in the lineup.

One of the things my team owner had stressed was the importance of everyone getting equal playing time. I reinforced this concept with the boys and explained that over the three-game series, if they started, they would play four or five innings, then come out. They liked the idea and came up with a great lineup, and we won our first series. The summer is long and injuries happen, so some players did get a little more playing time, but all in all, every player did their time at the position their college coach wanted, a few got to play other positions they wanted to improve at, and more than a few got to come in and pitch when we were short on pitchers. We lost in the first round of the playoffs, which sucked because we had the ability to win it all.

In game two of the three-game series, my third baseman was ejected in the top of the ninth inning for cussing at the umpire after a really badly called third strike. The team went nuts, as did my assistant coach. Because my third baseman got ejected, he was suspended for the next game, which meant his summer season had just come to an abrupt end. The ride home that night was not as jovial as it usually was. I knew the boys were upset with me, but that was okay.

The drive up the next day was better but not good. After we got to the field, I gave the boys a few minutes to stretch and get loose before they started their pregame routines. I called everyone into the dugout and shared my philosophy with them, explaining that from my vantage point, losing my composure would have been the wrong thing. Our player was in the wrong—he'd lost his composure, and in our league, unlike during the regular season, you cannot get away with saying stuff to the umpire.

More important, I stressed, was emulating behavior that I expected of them as men, husbands, and fathers in the future. I used examples of being newly married and coming home after a long, hard day at work, only to find out that your stay-at-home wife didn't have dinner ready. Would it be okay for you to yell, cuss, or say something demeaning because you expected dinner to be ready?

I further stressed the point by painting a picture of them having a five-year-old boy a few years later. I told them to imagine they got home and still had work to do, so after dinner, they were banging away on their laptop when their little boy threw a ball, spilling a drink all over the laptop. Would it be okay to lose your temper with your son? To yell, scream, belittle, or frighten him for being a child?

I wanted to stress that as *men*, we need to be in total control of our emotions, to be the thermostat, and to demonstrate positive behavior. Are there situations that warrant elevating your voice and taking up space? Sure, but those situations are and should be few and far between. Your spouse and children should feel comfortable around you, should look to you when something bad happens. If you can't control yourself or your emotions, you become difficult to follow, and you set the tone for how your children will respond and behave.

This calmly conveyed message really resonated with them, and I was proud to have the chance to not only coach them but to teach them important life lessons.

I love coaching. I love the nuances of the game, the opportunity to instruct, to learn about people, to experience highs and lows, and to live differently than most people ever get to live. Coaching provided me the opportunity to do something I had been missing since I was in the military—make a positive impact on the lives of others. And I wouldn't trade those experiences for the world.

The Gravy Sandwich Principle

You want to talk about leadership? Let me ask you this: How was that gravy sandwich you had on your last field exercise? You probably remember why you ate it. Because leaders eat last.

You made sure your soldiers were fed. You watched the skinny guy, making sure he had a full plate. You kept an eye on the bigger guy, ensuring he wasn't starving himself to pass tape.

And when you finally got to the line? You grabbed a piece of dry ass bread, poured some gravy on it, and called it a meal.

And it was fine. It was probably even delicious. Because the Joes ate first.

Leaders don't just say they care. They show it.

The Veteran's Edge Isn't Just Tactical—It's Moral

We lead from the front. Last one on and first one off the bird. Into the unknown.

We don't ask others to do what we won't. And we don't take credit when the mission succeeds. We build people. We take the hit. We finish the job.

That's not soft. That's elite. And in a world that's starving for character and competence? That's your edge.

Reflection and Recon

- Where in your life could you start leading again—without needing permission?
- Who taught you the value of empathy over authority?

- Where in your life today are you still trying to "prove" instead of connect?
- How would your relationships shift if you asked one more question and gave one less answer?

Call to Action: Practice Presence . . . Then Pass It On

Choose one person today—a spouse, teammate, client, or friend.

Instead of offering advice, ask them a question that gets below the surface:

- "How are you really doing?"
- "What's been weighing on you lately?"
- "What's one thing you wish people understood about what you're going through?"

Then listen. Just listen.

And when you're done? Do one more thing.

This particular exercise I first experienced at a conference, during a keynote given by Ashley Adamson. I'm not name dropping (per se LOL)—I just don't want to take credit for something I didn't come up with. Ashley is one of those rare people who can see right into the heart of a room—offering kindness without pity, truth without judgment. She is an incredible human being. Her words stayed with me long after I left, and they helped inform the message of this book.

Text someone who gave you advice that helped shape where you are today. Thank them. Let them know they made a difference.

It could be a coach, a teacher, a fellow veteran, a leader, a friend. Keep it simple: "Hey—just wanted you to know that something you told me once helped get me to where I am today. I'm grateful for it—and for you."

That's presence. That's empathy in action.

Because no one cares how much you know—until they know how much you care. And sometimes, caring starts with the courage to reach back—before you move forward.

CHAPTER 8

IN THE ARENA

"Never be lacking in zeal, but keep your spiritual fervor, serving the Lord." —Romans 12:11 (NIV)

My Story: Finding My Faith

Understanding the importance my faith plays in my life today requires a Tolkien- or Tarantino-like journey from the end, with a glimpse of what is going on right now. My faith is the foundation of my being, but it wasn't always this way. I was (and still am) a sinner, a self-centered and selfish person. I work earnestly to bypass those flaws and live like Christ commanded, to love my neighbors as I would love myself. I am in my mid-forties, and for the first time, I am making a conscious effort to learn, grow, and walk with the Lord every day.

Much like most things in my life, I have had an on-again, off-again relationship with church. When I was little and lived with my dad, we would go to a Methodist church. I recall going to one in Centerville, Virginia. My dad loves telling stories about how the pastor, who was an avid football fan, wore team socks of the then–Washington Redskins under his robe. He'd flash them for a hot second during the season just to rile the congregation up. I'm pretty sure I got baptized in that church when I was around six years old.

I don't remember where we went to church in New York—we lived there for less than a year—but I know when we moved to Michigan in late 1989, we went to St. Paul's United Methodist Church in Rochester. I loved it—it was big and grand with lots of people, and it had a good Sunday school program.

I remember being old enough to stay in church with my parents and learning the Apostles' Creed. It took me months to memorize it; I would open the hymnal to where it was and try to recall what line was coming next. Once I got one stanza down, I learned the next, and so on. I was so proud of myself the first time I was able to recite it fully from memory.

When I was old enough, I got to be an acolyte. If you don't know, acolytes are young people in the congregation who help with different parts of the service. I was in Cub Scouts and played sports, so I enjoyed putting on a "uniform" and getting to be in "the game." I didn't do much—we would light and extinguish the candles—but it was better than just sitting in the pews. I enjoyed having a defined purpose.

When I moved in the middle of sixth grade to live with my mom in California, we didn't go to church. I did look forward to visiting my dad in the summer or on holidays because it meant I'd get to go. Incidentally, my mom returned to her faith probably twenty years ago and is a devout Catholic. She and her late husband—my stepdad, Robert—were heavily involved in their parish, and my mom still is to this day.

I moved back to my dad's in the middle of my junior year of high school. He, my stepmom, and my brothers had found a Presbyterian church closer to home. I liked it and got involved in youth group and choir as soon as I moved back.

In my senior year, I met my first wife. We were in youth group and choir together, and our pastor is the one who married us. Our first "date" was on Christmas Eve 1998. We were part of a trio singing "O Who's That Yonder," and I asked if she wanted to hang out between the 10 p.m. and midnight services.

Technically, my first coaching gig came in the summer after I graduated high school, as I volunteered to run the sports program of the church's vacation Bible school during the summer. After that, I went to college, where I failed out after my freshman year, then moved to Washington (the state) to live with my mom and eventually joined the army.

Unfortunately, like most young men in their late teens and early twenties, God was not a big part of my life. He was a footnote at best and mainly gave me a guilty conscience at Christmas and Easter. I was more focused on getting drunk and chasing girls than following my faith.

My first interaction with God came while we were in Kuwait waiting to push across the border to Iraq in January or February 2004. My best friend found out that his wife (at the time) had been pregnant and lost the baby. I asked if I could pray for him, and a handful of us went outside the tent, wrapped our arms around each other, and prayed. I don't know what I prayed, but I do recall having my eyes closed, and I could see us from about fifteen feet above. It was definitely an out-of-body experience, with the scene painted like a desert sunset—wild pinks, blues, and purples with streaks of silver and white. Like an apparition floating above in a first-person role-playing video game, I could see the scene in real time. When we all said "amen," the vision dissolved, and I was back in my body.

As I have mentioned, I deployed a total of six times, three of them in combat zones. I came home relatively unscathed, with all my fingers and toes, both eyes, both ears, my nose, my legs, and my arms. I was no worse for wear, and looking back, that is certainly by the grace of God. Especially after counter–improvised explosive device (C-IED) systems were installed in our vehicles, we'd come back from a mission, do a check, and see if we had any "missed calls," which meant there had been an attempt by someone to remote detonate an IED, but the C-IED system had worked and jammed the signal.

I had quite a few missed calls. During my first trip to Iraq, we were in An Najaf, and there was a pretty decent sniper in the area. Somewhere I have a picture of one of the view blocks from my M1117 armored security vehicle with a bullet impact mark right where my head would have been. Same thing with my driver. Thank you, Cadillac, Mercedes, and Textron, for making such an incredible vehicle and strong view blocks!

There was another time in An Najaf where we had just parked our Humvee after a mission when we started taking indirect fire. Less than two minutes after we parked it, a mortar went right through the gunner's turret and decimated the entire inside of our truck.

After the out-of-body experience while praying, the next significant encounter with my faith came when my son was baptized in December 2007. He was six months old, and I was deploying to Iraq for the second time in a few weeks. My best friend was his godfather, and my ex-wife's sister was his godmother. We had a simple but memorable baptism at the same church we had met in twelve years earlier. I felt an odd, warm sensation, like I was being hugged during the ceremony, and I felt a tightness in my chest—literally something tugging at my heart.

Very little in terms of combat happened during that deployment. I returned in March 2009 and was on orders to Fort Campbell that summer. When we moved there, my ex-wife wanted to find a church to get involved with. This is what I consider the starting line of my current walk in faith.

We attended New Work Fellowship. It was an incredible nondenominational church. I was hesitant at first because other nondenominational churches I had attended never felt like church; there was a lot of preaching but very little about God. But the worship team at New Work Fellowship was awesome. The music was great and even masculine at times.

As units from the 101st started coming down on orders, they began doing a thing at the end of each service where they would share the names and ranks of people deployed whose family had asked for prayers. I knew I wanted that. Afghanistan was going to be a different beast than Iraq, and I could use all the help I could get.

On Easter Sunday 2010, I decided to get baptized again as an adult. I was still an infant in my understanding and stewardship of my faith, but I wanted to make a conscious decision as an adult to give my life to Jesus.

I experienced a few exciting events while in Afghanistan and, arrogantly, decided it was my effectiveness as an experienced combat leader that allowed me and my soldiers to return home. We moved to Germany after Fort Campbell; nothing significant from a religious standpoint to report on there. After that, I got orders to Fort Bragg, where I had the opportunity to be a paratrooper, something I had been chasing for sixteen years since basic training.

At Fort Bragg, we attended Manna Church, another nondenominational church built along "the military highway," as they said. This was the first time I took my faith seriously as an adult. This church 100 percent preached from the Bible and prided itself on getting those who would never enter a church to become believers.

The head pastor shared a story about a young woman whose profession was obviously being a lady of the night. She found her way to the church doors, dressed in a too-tight dress with parts of her spilling out, her hair a mess, with a totally disheveled air about her. The looks and hushed accusations and judgment flowed through the congregation like ripples on a pond after a rock is thrown.

At this point in the story, I was very self-righteous. I grew up in proper churches as a kid; you always wore your Sunday best, had your hair combed, and wore dress shoes. I was about to get served some humble pie, as the preacher explained that a few elders saw her and welcomed her in with open arms. They found a trench coat she could cover herself up with, got her some coffee, and sat with her in the back. They didn't let the judgment of the congregation scare her away. Instead, they showed her what God's love and church really is—welcoming and nonjudgmental.

The pastor shared that the pastor at the time admonished the congregation a bit, for the woman was a prime example of who they were trying to reach—someone who would usually never set foot near a church, let alone in one. As Christians, they were called to seek out the poor, the fallen, the wretched, and bring them back to their Father's house.

That is just one of many examples where my preconceived notions and self-righteousness have been squashed by the word of God.

The lesson I took away that day has been repeated and shared with me over and over, and it's been boiled down to one sentence, reinforced by Jesus' disciples: *God doesn't call the qualified; He qualifies the called.* This is the single most important lesson I have learned during my walk with the Lord. We are all loved; we are all *worthy* of His love. But we have to be willing to accept that, and for our tiny, human brains, especially mine, that can be a truth that is very hard to fathom.

That's a lesson I learned the hard way a few weeks later. There was a major community event at the main campus in Fayetteville. There was going to be live worship music, small-group presentations, food, childcare, and more. At the end of the night, I was jacked up—my Holy Spirit meter was pegged. We all circled around some elders and prayed over them, arms and hands extended. The pastor said, "Let the Holy Spirit move through you," as we prayed over them. Guess what happened?! NOTHING. No electric charge, no "Spidey" sense, no spiritual warm hug. I felt nothing. I can look back now and realize I was looking for a sign, for God to prove to ME (arrogant!) that He existed—if the Holy Spirit would just give me a nudge and say, "Hey, bud, that was me. I'm real!" *Then* I could really believe.

That was in 2019, before my last deployment. I kept a lukewarm faith for the next few years. I'd remember to pray now and then and make a more conscious effort to understand and celebrate the real reasons for Christmas and Easter, but really, I was just a part-time Christian buying tickets to a few home games. I wasn't even a season ticket holder, and I certainly didn't have the intestinal fortitude to suit up and try out for the team.

During and after my divorce, I found a small church down the street from my home in Michigan, but it wasn't the right feel. It wasn't until Caitlyn and I were a few months out from getting married that we found the church that would propel us into our faith. When I left my dream job of coaching baseball at Hillsdale College, I was clearly working through a lot of stuff but at least had the wherewithal to understand that I needed God's help; I was trying to do too much on my own.

There was a "mega" church ten minutes away. I put mega in quotations because, yes, it is on a large campus, holds huge events, and has thousands of attendees, but it has never felt fake like other mega churches do. I'm talking about Northridge Church in Plymouth, Michigan, led by a brilliant follower of Jesus named Brad and supported by many other phenomenal pastors.

We found a home in Northridge. The first service we attended, Levi was giving the sermon, and in the middle, I felt something tugging at my heart. I started crying. It wasn't uncontrollable sobbing but a steady stream of tears. The message had resonated so strongly with me. The essence of it was: "How many signs do we need until we learn to trust and obey God?"

See, the previous few weeks, I'd interviewed twice at Cabrini. I knew I'd crushed it and was offered the job. But a few days before going to Northridge, I had rejected the job offer from Cabrini because it had been posted as a full-time job when, in reality, it was a part-time job that only paid a small stipend. However, they had come back and offered a full-time *teaching* position.

My wife knew exactly what I was feeling when she saw my face and said, "You're going to take the job, aren't you?" Through tears, I laughed and said, "Yes, I am." I called the assistant director and said, "If the teaching job is still on the table, I'd like to accept both the coaching and teaching positions."

Three weeks later, I was anxiously waiting for my first-period students to come through the door. Almost exactly one year later, on October 13, 2024, my wife gave her life to Jesus and was baptized at Northridge Church. It was an incredible day and moment for her and our family, one that we didn't know would have such a profound effect.

In the summer of 2024, I left my job at Cabrini for an incredible opportunity, which would require us to move to Arizona. I had a strong feeling my son was going to get accepted to Grand Canyon University, the largest private Christian university in the country, which was thirty to forty minutes from where we would live. So I was less concerned about it impacting my relationship with him, as he would be okay with the proximity and more than happy to spread his wings.

However, I knew when I accepted the job that it was going to severely strain the relationship with my daughter. The divorce was extremely tough for her. Even though we lived only a mile apart, it might as well have been on the other side of the country, and here I was, literally turning that into a reality. As expected, she was distant, sometimes rude, and even a bit hurtful at times. But Caitlyn, who is incredibly close with my daughter, and I did our best to not only tell her but *show* her how important and special she was in our lives and how much we loved her. Both Caitlyn and I prayed for patience and strength to endure the emotional distress in our lives. We prayed for my daughter to see, understand, know, and feel that she was loved by us. Slowly but surely, she began to understand, and our relationship improved.

In January 2025, I enlisted the help and coaching services of Pete, who is our favorite pastor at Northridge. He is very well spoken, kind, and genuine, and when it's his sermon, you know it's going to be good. He delivers his messages in a way that makes them feel like they were crafted for you. In one sermon, he mentioned he was a life coach, so I reached out. I was new to a job in finance that was going to make a significant impact on the fiscal future of my family and would take a toll on my mental and emotional health. I was still in the license-earning phase and wanted to make the most out of the time and flexibility I had then to improve myself in as many areas as I could.

I couldn't have asked for a better life coach. Pete got me ready to take on the world I was so close to entering full time. He helped identify and defeat (or at least mitigate the damage from) the blind spots and weaknesses I had in my spiritual, mental, and emotional lives. The growth I experienced under his tutelage was exponential and life-changing. I would not be writing this book or reaping its benefits without Pete. He has become a very close friend over the last year, and I am so grateful he took the time to hear my story and bring me on as a client.

Unbeknownst to me and Caitlyn, because we took my daughter to church with us when it was our weekend with the kids, she had started to see things differently. My daughter had slowly been finding her faith and the truth, and she ultimately told us she wanted to get baptized.

On April 6, 2025, my daughter gave her life to Jesus Christ and was baptized at Northridge Church. That morning, she handed me a handwritten note apologizing for how she had treated me the last several months and explaining I was the reason she believed in God and wanted to get baptized. I completely lost it—there's no better gift than that, in my opinion. Juliana has grown into quite the prayer warrior; she holds Bible studies with her friends and shares lessons on TikTok and Instagram, and we are even looking into starting a YouTube channel for her.

I can hardly express the pride I have in Juliana's faith journey, and it is incredibly humbling to know that I played a part in it. That's the power of God's love and grace. By connecting with Him, we connect with each other too. And that's something I will always be grateful for.

The People Who Saw Through It

As you've read, I had my fair share of challenges after retiring from the army and embarking on my new journey as a civilian. But I had something a lot of guys don't: "Whose car we takin'?" friends. That line from *The Town* says it all. Four guys I trust with my life. Guys I don't have to pretend with. Guys who would call me out when I started putting the mask back on.

When I started dating my now wife, she saw through it too. She encouraged me to talk to someone. To really talk.

I reached out to the VA. And I got lucky—I was matched with a counselor who understood me. And for four months, I got better.

But that's the thing: Because I wasn't "bad enough," wasn't considering hurting myself or someone else, I didn't qualify for long-term, one-on-one care. So after progress came . . . regression.

The struggle wasn't chaos or collapse. It was repetition. I was doing the same things over and over again, making small tweaks, hoping for a different outcome. From the outside, it looked like progress. Inside, it felt like stagnation.

I felt hollow. Empty. Not broken but not whole either. I could tell something was missing, even if I didn't have the language for it yet. There was a quiet absence that followed me through otherwise normal days, a sense that I was going through the motions of a life that no longer fit.

What made it harder was the reluctance to admit what that absence might be. Like Adam in Genesis, I was hiding—not because I didn't believe in God but because I was afraid of Him. Afraid of being seen clearly. Afraid that if I stood fully exposed, I would find disappointment instead of grace. So I stayed busy. I stayed distracted. I stayed just close enough to avoid confronting what I already knew was missing.

I slipped. Slowly.

Until we found our church. And everything changed.

When Belonging Returned

The change didn't come in a flash of light or some overnight breakthrough. As you've read, it started quietly, back at my church in Michigan—through the steady mentorship of my pastor. But it really took hold after my wife and I moved to Arizona.

The opening message on the screen was from Romans 12:10–12. One line stopped me cold: "Never be lacking in zeal, but keep your spiritual fervor, serving the Lord."

I realized I hadn't felt zeal—true passion and drive—since the day I took the uniform off.

Then came the sermon series: "In the Arena". It opened with President Teddy Roosevelt's "The Man in the Arena" speech, which I'll delve into more shortly. The whole message hit me like a freight train: Stop being a spectator. Start being a contributor. Step into the arena.

As a former athlete and coach, that metaphor cut straight to the heart. And then the final point drove it all the way home: Service is the ultimate calling. My pastor told the story of Jesus washing the feet of His disciples—including Judas, the one who would betray Him. Even in that moment, Jesus chose service.

That's when it clicked for me: The real way forward isn't about chasing status or recreating the past. It's about service. When I serve, I live.

My Story: Out of the Stands, In the Arena

The move to Arizona was executed in two phases. In phase one, I packed up my truck with as much stuff as I could, drove it from Michigan to Arizona, unloaded it in the garage, and flew back. Phase two involved having a garage sale, packing up the remainder of our belongings into a pod, and loading the dogs and our suitcases into Caitlyn's SUV. Then the four of us made the four-day trek to our new home. Unfortunately, a couple of weeks later, the job that I had moved to Arizona for fell through.

For the third straight summer, I was unemployed. This time, I was devastated. I'd picked a completely new career field, one that I was bound to be really good at, one that was going to enable me to create generational wealth.

It's funny how God's timing and blessing (even when it doesn't feel that way at the time) is immaculate. It took a couple of weeks and dinner with some of Caitlyn's friends in Arizona, but we found a church. They had all recommended Christ Church of the Valley (CCV). I had no idea what I was in store for, but I can picture God in heaven, one hand on His hip, the other over a smile, watching and chuckling as He put me right where I needed to be.

The first service we attended at CCV was week two of their summer series called "In the Arena." Teddy Roosevelt is hands down my favorite president and probably my favorite American. The speech "The Man in the Arena" is an all-time top three speech, in my opinion. In the sermon, the head pastor, Ashley—who is an incredible man and pastor, by the way—talked about lukewarm Christians and Christianity and how we needed to be "the man in the arena."

He equated it to being an athlete. He said most of us are just attending the game now and then. Sometimes we get lucky and get to sit in the VIP boxes, but really, that's the extent of our participation—just watching, not doing anything. He said there are some who eventually suit up, but they just sit on the sidelines. They don't do anything that impacts the game. It's like, "Hey, I'm wearing the uniform—I'm part of the team." Technically, yes, but in reality, are you? Then he said, "The vast *minority* are on the field. They are in there, mixing it up, trying to make a difference. The ones in the stands, the ones in the VIP boxes, even the ones on the bench—they're lukewarm Christians. We don't need lukewarm Christians; we need red-hot Christians. Followers of Christ who aren't afraid to get in the arena." Then he presented the following portion of the speech, and that really nailed what it means to be a Christian who isn't on the sideline anymore:

"The credit belongs to the man who is actually in the arena, whose face is marred by dust and sweat and blood, who strives valiantly, who errs, who comes short again and again because there is no effort without error and shortcoming, but who does actually strive to do the deeds; who knows great enthusiasms, the great devotions; who spends himself in a worthy cause."[1]

Tell me that isn't a damn near perfect explanation of what it means to be a follower of Christ. You're going to work hard, you're going to get beat up and bloodied, you are going to try over and over and fail over and over because we are all sinners. And the only thing that can save you is to believe in and give your life to Jesus . . . a worthy cause.

[1] Woolridge, Ashley. "Christianity Isn't a Spectator Sport." Sermon. Christ's Church of the Valley, Phoenix, AZ, on August 16, 2025.

This time, the tears that streamed down my face *were* uncontrollable. For the first time in my life, I knew what it meant and what it would take to be a follower of Jesus Christ.

I have experienced that high and those emotions several times as we have attended services at CCV. Ashley and all the other pastors preach from the Bible, they call out sin, they challenge us to recognize where we fall short in our lives and our pursuit of Jesus, but they also remind us that it's okay to fail—and really, it's expected for us to fail because Jesus was the only person who lived a perfect life. And then He endured an unimaginably violent, horrific death at the very hands of the people who were created in His/His Father's image, solely for the purpose of absolving us from our sins, asking only that we believe in Him.

See, this is where and why Christianity stands out and above all other religions. Forget the fact that other religions acknowledge Jesus, His disciples, and the places and events listed in various books of the Bible, which is a historically accurate document. Christianity is the only religion that does not have a checklist or a to-do list to get into heaven. Jesus is the way, the truth, and the life. All you have to do is believe in Him, give your heart to Him, and love your neighbor as you would love yourself. The key, however, is this cannot be a one-time, isolated event. It must be a constant, conscious decision repeated over and over. And when you fail, which you undoubtedly will, you repent, ask for forgiveness, and try again.

In late August 2025, I'd been in Arizona for almost two full months and hadn't heard back from a single job I had applied for—and let me tell you, I had applied to dozens over the previous several weeks. I'd started writing as a means of getting my mind off being unemployed and had started drafting a fiction book in the military/spy thriller genre dominated by my favorite authors, Jack Carr and Brad Thor. I'd written four chapters over the last few days and shared them with a few friends and family, and they were chomping at the bit. One of my best friends, a self-admitted nonreader, told me he couldn't wait for the next chapter—he was enthralled by the book so far and encouraged me to keep it up.

On Sunday, August 7, 2025, the sermon at CCV was about using the gifts God gave you. To be a good steward of said gifts to enhance other people's lives and draw people closer to Him and His kingdom.

The next day, I sat at the dining room table and prayed harder than I ever had in my life. For a solid fifteen minutes, and it wasn't pretty. I had tears streaming down my face. My eyes were red and swollen, sensitive to the touch. I am pretty sure I had snot bubbles too, as my allergies were in full effect. I prayed out loud, asking God for direction and guidance while also thanking Him for the love, grace, and mercy He had blessed me with that I did not deserve. I asked Him for a clear sign—not a hint or a nudge but a Kevin-proof, unmistakable sign about what He wanted me to do with my life.

Less than an hour later, my phone rang. I looked down and saw it was Pete, my friend and life coach. He told me he felt like God wanted him to call me and talk to me. He said he'd read some of my writing and asked what my plans were. I admitted I wasn't sure. He said he felt that God had put it on his heart to tell me to pursue writing. I told him I had just finished praying for a clear sign, and here he was delivering it. Talk about a God moment!

Since that moment, I have pursued writing with an unwavering belief that I am following God's vision for my life. While not on the same scale of scope, difficulty, or impact as Taylor Swift's Eras Tour, I embarked on a significant undertaking: planning a forty-plus-city nationwide book tour from Memorial Day to Veterans Day 2026. It's America's 250th birthday, and my book is designed to help veterans, the men and women who stood in the gap and said, "Here I am, Lord, send me." The magnitude of the book tour is far beyond anything I can handle on my own, which my CCV campus pastor, Cooper, said points to it being God driven, as it will require me to lean on Him and not on myself to make it happen.

I also found a publishing team who believed in me, my book, and my message. That publishing team is Ballast Books, and they have been so incredible and supportive in not only bringing my vision to life but doing so in a manner that is professional, marketable, and meaningful without removing the authenticity or heart of my work. So much so, in fact, the stories that are shared throughout the book are based on their suggestion to build a stronger rapport with you, the reader, and draw you in even more, so my story becomes *our* story, a shared journey of trials, tribulations, and triumphs. Sounds like another story I've read—of a baby born in Bethlehem who lived through trials and tribulations and, after rising from the dead three days after his crucifixion, provided the greatest triumph the world has ever known.

What I'd Tell the One Still Struggling Silently

If you're reading this, and you're wearing the same mask I used to . . . listen to me: Know who your people are.

The fake friends. The lukewarm family. They cannot help you.

But when you know who the real ones are, do not shut them out. If they are real, they will ride for you. They will fight for you. They will walk through hell to get to you. So let them in.

Because you would have done it for them. Without question.

And here is the part I did not understand for a long time. Connection isn't only horizontal. It is also vertical.

Even with the right people around you, there will be moments when no one fully understands what you are carrying. When the weight feels too personal. Too heavy. Too quiet.

For me, that is where faith entered the picture. Not as a sermon. Not as a rulebook. But as a relationship.

I did not find God when life was going well. I found Him when I ran out of places to hide. When I couldn't put the mask back on. When the silence got loud enough that I finally asked for help.

And what I found was not judgment—it was presence.

If you are not religious, I am not asking you to believe anything right now. I am simply asking you to consider this: You were never meant to carry everything alone. Not from your family. Not from your friends. Not in your soul.

For me, that realization led me to Jesus. Not because someone argued me into faith but because I needed a connection that did not break under pressure.

You may not be there yet, and that's okay. But if you are searching for something deeper than distraction, stronger than willpower, and more constant than people, do not ignore that pull.

Let your people in.

And stay open to the possibility that there is someone else who already sees you fully, knows what you are carrying, and is ready to walk through it with you.

Reflection and Recon

- What does your silence sound like?
- What masks are you still wearing—around family, friends, or even yourself?
- Who are your "Whose car we takin'?" people?
- Are you pushing away the very people who want to help you heal?

Call to Action: Break the Silence—One Sentence at a Time

Sometimes the heaviest step is the smallest one.

Tonight, have the courage to reach out. Send a text, make a call, or FaceTime someone who matters. It doesn't have to be a long story. It doesn't have to be a dramatic reveal. Just something along the lines of, "I've been carrying more than I let on. I don't need you to fix it—I just don't want to carry it alone anymore."

Send it to someone who sees you. Or someone you want to see again.

Because the silence doesn't protect you—it isolates you. And you are not meant to do this alone.

CHAPTER 10

LEAVING A LEGACY THAT SPEAKS

"A life is not important except in the impact it has on other lives." —Jackie Robinson

My Story: My New Mission

Today, my life is quieter than it used to be. There is no formation to fall into. No rank on my chest. No mission briefing telling me exactly where to be and what to do next.

And yet, for the first time in a long time, it feels grounded.

I am not finished. There are still challenges. There are still days when the weight shows up unannounced. But I am no longer lost. I am no longer invisible to myself. And that matters.

For a long time, the part of me that had to die so I could move forward was the belief that being a soldier was all that I was. The military was a great foundation. A powerful stepping stone. It gave me discipline, purpose, brotherhood, and tools that shaped who I am. But it was never meant to be the end of my story.

I still have a lot of life to live.

One of the most important shifts I made was returning to a mindset I once lived by as a squad leader at my best. Extreme ownership. No excuses. No blame. When things go wrong, it starts with me. That does not mean other people do not play a role. It means I choose responsibility over resentment. Ownership over bitterness. Growth over stagnation.

Another hard lesson was learning to stop expecting myself out of other people. I still believe in people. I still expect good things. But not everyone carries the same depth of compassion or empathy, and holding them to my internal standard only created frustration. That realization hurt, but it freed me.

Faith plays a quiet but steady role in my life now. It shows up in prayer before meals. In trying to start and end my day with intention. In reading Scripture, even when it does not immediately make sense. Faith is no longer about asking and receiving. It is about patience. About believing in something I cannot touch or see, but trusting that it will work out in the end.

God has taught me patience in the silence in a way success never could.

I realized I was not being abandoned, just reshaped, the day I broke down crying at the table last August. That moment did not feel holy. It felt raw. But looking back, it marked a turning point. Something was being rebuilt.

I show up differently for my children now. I am more intentional than I have ever been. I hope they remember that they saw me get knocked down, take the standing eight, and step back into the fight. Not blindly. Not recklessly. But with belief. In myself. In my mission. In my message. And in God.

Some relationships in my life have deepened. Former friends have become close again. Others have fallen away. That is part of the process. The work I do now, the words I choose, and the presence I bring are aimed squarely at veterans.

This book, and the work surrounding it, are my way of staying in the fight. Not for attention. Not for recognition. But for proximity. Writing this book was about giving language to experiences many veterans struggle to name. Author events and speaking engagements are simply an extension of that same intent. To sit across from people. To listen. To remind them they are not alone, not broken, and not disqualified from a meaningful next chapter. The legacy I am working to build is not measured in sales, stages, or applause. It is measured in quiet moments when someone feels seen, steadied, and willing to keep going.

If you are reading this and that sounds like you, hear me clearly.

You are not too far gone. You are not disqualified. And you are not done.

I want you to feel seen. Heard. Worthy. And hopeful. No matter what you have said or done. No matter what bridges you have burned. If you own your part and make an earnest effort, you can still move forward. You can still build a meaningful, beautiful life.

When my kids are grown, I hope they say I modeled tenacity. Resilience. Hard work. Discipline. And empathy.

If people become better leaders because they crossed paths with me, I hope they are rational, selfless, competent, and confident. Leaders who do the work quietly. Leaders who stay steady when things get hard.

If my legacy could be summed up in one sentence, it would be this.

I will take the over on the underdog.

Today, my life speaks without a uniform or title by choosing patience over panic. By doing the work that needs to be done, even when no one is watching. By believing in myself. By trusting the process. And by learning to enjoy the journey instead of rushing past it.

Legacy does not wait for the end. It is built in the daily decisions to keep going, to stay honest, and to live in a way that leaves others better than you found them.

That is the life I am building now.

The Mirror and the Mission

There comes a moment—quiet, unavoidable—when you look in the mirror and ask, *Who am I now?*

Not the uniform. Not the rank. Not the medals or deployments. Just you. Stripped down. No orders. No battle rhythm. No saluting.

And at first? That reflection might scare you. Because for so long, your identity was the mission. You knew who you were by the patch on your shoulder and the people who counted on you. Now . . . you're not sure what you're building. Or who you're building it for.

But here's the truth I had to learn the hard way (and that I've shared with you throughout this book): The mission never left. It just changed uniforms.

You still have strength. You still have wisdom. You still have a voice. You're just being asked to lead in a different way now. Not through orders—but through presence. Not through rank—but through relationships. Not in a duty station—but in your home, your workplace, your community. That shift starts in the mirror.

You have to reclaim yourself before you can serve others again. And that's not weak. That's warrior-level work.

Becoming Unrecognizable—Then Unstoppable

A few months ago, I sat across from my pastor and life coach. I had entered a new phase of my life, one where I wasn't just trying to rebuild—I was trying to create impact on a much larger scale. And I had to ask myself a question I'd spent years avoiding: *Who am I . . . really?*

Not the soldier. Not the coach. Not the teacher. Not the title. Just . . . me.

And what I saw in that mirror wasn't shame. It was unfinished.

I saw someone who needed help. Who needed guidance. Who was being called into something bigger but wasn't quite ready yet. That conversation changed my life.

It reminded me that the mission moving forward isn't about proving I matter—it's about living like I already do.

The Trap of Performance-Based Identity

For most of my life, my identity was tied to what I did. In the army, it was rank and responsibility. As a coach and teacher, it was about leadership and results. Even at Hillsdale College, surrounded by one of the most special coaching staff and incredible student athletes, it wasn't enough.

I needed a better title. More recognition. More prestige.

And even after I left Hillsdale and had the privilege to be the head coach at the high school level, it still wasn't enough. I thought, *Maybe I need to get back to college baseball.*

Because that sounded better. Looked better. Felt more impressive. But nothing external ever filled the void. What finally changed?

I stopped chasing status and started chasing service.

That's why this book and helping my fellow veterans matters to me and keeps me up at night—in the best way.

Because it's not about me anymore. It's about what I can do for others.

The Shift from Success to Significance

Maybe it started when I met Caitlyn and fell in love. But I didn't fully embrace it until I stepped into a career outside my comfort zone—one where I could help people every day and lay the foundation for something bigger.

I stopped chasing promotions and started chasing purpose. I realized that transformation doesn't begin with a title.

It begins with truth. And sometimes that truth stares you in the mirror with no rank, no patch, no applause—and asks you to show up anyway.

What I'd Say to the Man in the Mirror Back Then

Of course you didn't recognize yourself. You were stepping into something new. Unknown. Uncomfortable.

You were becoming.

Just like a caterpillar transforms into a butterfly, your spirit already knew what your mind couldn't yet understand. You were built for more—not more applause. More impact.

This isn't your end. It's your emergence.

Reflection and Recon

- When was the last time you looked in the mirror and saw someone becoming something greater, not less?
- Are you chasing status . . . or purpose?

- What's one thing you've been telling yourself you need to achieve before you matter? Is it true?

Call to Action: Name Your Mission Statement

Tonight, write this sentence down at the top of a page:

"The man/woman I'm becoming is . . ."

Then list three truths about who you are becoming—not what you do but who you are when no one's looking.

Examples:

- A person who builds people up.
- A servant leader who listens and leads with strength.
- A legacy-maker—not just for his family but for the next generation.

Don't worry about perfect words. This isn't for show; it's for you. You're not reporting for duty anymore. You're stepping into your calling.

And later in this journey, you'll write something bigger: the legacy you want to leave behind—the words you'd want spoken when your story's done.

But today? Just start with who you're becoming. Because the future starts there.

Establishing Your Legacy

There's a moment every veteran faces—quiet and often alone—when you wonder if it all mattered. Not just the years in uniform. But you. Who you were before the military. Who you became during it. And who you are now that the noise has stopped.

We spend so much time being what others need us to be: The leader. The strong one. The provider. The protector.

And when the uniform comes off, we're left asking, *Did I leave a mark that matters?*

But here's what I know: You're still here. Which means the mission isn't over. And neither is your legacy.

Too many of us are waiting for someone else to tell our story. Waiting for a retirement speech . . . Waiting for the eulogy . . . Waiting for the world to finally notice what we carried.

But brother/sister—don't wait. Don't wait for the end to start building something that speaks. Start now.

Speak life into your home. Lead with honor in your community. Give others permission to heal by showing them how you did it first. Because this is how legacy is built—not in titles or trophies but in moments. In presence. In consistency. In showing up with purpose when no one's watching.

The world doesn't need another highlight reel. It needs your story. Your scars. Your strength. It needs to hear from the man who came home and found his voice again. From the woman who carried the weight and still chose to lift others up.

And if no one has told you this yet—let me be the first: You are not invisible. You are a force. And your best chapter might just be the one you haven't written yet.

So don't sit back quietly. Speak. Lead. Live. Because the way you walk from here will echo far beyond you.

That's legacy. That's the mission now. And brother/sister . . . you're ready.

The Foxhole Just Got Bigger

In the military, we had a simple phrase: "Improve your foxhole." It meant leaving your position better than you found it. Stronger. Safer. More secure. Better camouflage. Better lines of sight. Interlocking fields of fire.

That phrase still applies. Only now, the foxhole is bigger—it's the world. Build it. Beautify it. Fortify it. For everyone coming after you.

Legacy isn't selfish. It's sacred. It's built in how you love your family. It's built in how you show up to your job. It's built in how you serve when no one sees it. It's built in how you forgive—and who you raise. It's built in the broken places you choose to heal—and in the hearts you help feel seen.

Legacy isn't about building statues or getting your name etched on a building. It's not ego. It's not fiction. Legacy is living your life in a way that helps someone else become the best version of themselves. It's standing on the shoulders of giants—and choosing to become one.

What I Want to Leave Behind

I don't need my kids to follow in my military footsteps. In fact, I hope they don't. It's hard. It takes a toll. But what I do want to leave behind is this: a life rooted in servant leadership.

Because Jesus washed feet.

That's the standard. Not titles. Not medals. Not applause.

My family will inherit more than assets. They'll inherit standards. They'll know what sacrifice looks like. They'll know what it means to love God, love people, and lead with grace and grit.

And for the veteran community—my community—I want to leave a mirror and a map. I've been in their boots. I know the dark rooms. I know the heavy silences. And I want to build something that helps them find their footing again. Not someday—now.

I Won't Wait for the Eulogy

A few years ago, I realized I didn't want to wait for people to say nice things about me after I was gone. I wanted them to feel those things while I was still here. So I started saying it. I started giving my time. I started forgiving more. Dreaming bigger. Loving louder.

Legacy isn't some future fantasy. It's how you show up today. And if you're waiting for permission to start?

Here it is.

But let's be clear: You never needed permission. You were born with purpose. You were forged in challenge.

You were designed to leave the world better than you found it.

If they stood up at your funeral tomorrow—what would they say? Not the prewritten niceties. The real words.

Would they say you made people feel valued? That you loved fiercely and unconditionally? That you served with passion and led with purpose? That you made the world better? That you pointed to something greater than yourself?

This isn't about dying. This is about deciding—how you want to be remembered and whether your life is aligned with that today.

You don't need permission. But here it is anyway: Live bold. Love hard. Forgive quickly. Build freely. Lead humbly. And never wait for the eulogy to say what matters most.

Medal of Honor recipient and recently reenlisted United States Marine Corps Sergeant Dakota Meyer said it best: "Your life is made up of two dates separated by a dash. Make the most out of the dash."

Reflection and Recon

- What story do you want your life to tell?
- Who do you need to tell "thank you" or "I love you"—before it's too late?
- What part of your life needs realignment with the legacy you want to leave?

Call to Action: Write Your Eulogy

Yes, right now. Not to be morbid. To be intentional.

Take fifteen minutes. Write what you hope they say when you're gone. Start with, "Today, we gather not just to mourn a loss but to honor a life . . ." Then answer:

- Who were you really?
- What did you stand for?
- Who did you love well?
- What did you fight for?
- What do you leave behind?

Don't wait. Start living the legacy now. Then go write the next chapter—off the page, out in the world.

Because your story isn't over. It's about to begin again.

Final Words

You are not invisible. You are indispensable. You are not behind. You're exactly where you need to be. And this world? It's your foxhole now. Improve it. Lead in it. Love in it.

And when your time here is done—let your legacy speak for itself.

A LETTER TO YOU, THE READER

From one veteran to another, if you're holding this book right now, I want you to know something: I see you. Not the rank. Not the ribbons. Not the résumé. You.

The man or woman who gave years of their life to something bigger than themselves. The one who carried weight without complaint. Who stood guard while others slept. Who came home and wondered where they went.

I wrote this book because I lived it. The silence. The drifting. The ache to belong again. The pride that clashed with the pain. The days I didn't feel like I mattered anymore—no mission, no map, no momentum.

But slowly, I realized something: The mission wasn't over. It had simply changed.

You're not meant to fade into the background. You're meant to lead—differently now, yes, but with just as much fire.

This book is your permission slip to stop apologizing for your story. To stop hiding your strength. To stop waiting for the world to understand you—and start reminding it who you are.

You are not invisible. You are indispensable. And the world still needs what only you can give. So go forward. Build. Speak. Mentor. Love. Leave something behind that echoes long after you're gone. And if you ever forget who you are? Come back to these pages. I'll be right here—reminding you.

With honor and brotherhood,

Kevin Kidder

ACKNOWLEDGMENTS

To my wife, Caitlyn: You are the best thing that has ever happened to me. You met me when I was in a dark place. You saw me. You believed in me when I didn't have much to offer you but my heart. You ruined my plans of becoming Clint Eastwood in *Gran Torino*, and I am so grateful you did. I love doing life with you and look forward to bugging you for the rest of our lives.

To my kids, Ty and Juliana: I love you so much and am so very proud of you. Of all the titles I mentioned in this book, none will ever compare to being called your dad. You are gifts from God and the greatest adventures of my life. I look forward to watching you grow into young adults and take on the world.

To my pastor and coach, Pete: Thank you for everything you have done for me. You helped me transition into this season of my life, encouraged me to write this book, and helped me see myself, all while strengthening my faith. I cannot thank you enough.

To my core four—K, Jason, Justin, and Jake: You guys are irreplaceable, and I cherish our friendship more than I could ever hope to explain in two lifetimes. You have been there for me through so many impactful moments in my life, good and bad, and you never swayed. You are the true definition of battle buddies, and I love you.

To Laffy: God's timing is impeccable. Brother, I am so grateful He brought us back into each other's lives. The intentionality with which you seek His heart is incredible. Your support of me and my endeavors is a gift I can't repay but that I will do my best to steward with intentionality and care. Your accountability via the Gospel is truly unwavering and emulates one of God's chosen.

To my parents: I am truly blessed to have you as my mom and dad. I would be hard-pressed to find someone who was loved as unconditionally as I was. Your values, your standards, and the example you set shaped me into who I am today. Although this book talks a lot about unpleasant feelings, you were always there for me, just a phone call or quick trip away. Your ever-present love is one of the biggest reasons I didn't succumb to those unpleasant feelings.

To my family: Thank you for all the love and support you have shown me over the years. I may be a rolling stone, but you have always reminded me that no matter where life takes me, home isn't a place—it's the people who refuse to let go of you.

To my fellow coaches: What you do is incredible. The time, energy, and focus you give of yourself to others in the pursuit of them becoming the best versions of themselves is incredible. Coaching puts you under the microscope in so many ways, but as long as you stay true to the mission—making a positive impact in the lives of others—let them look on fondly.

To my former players and soldiers: I love you dearly. I cherished our time together, and even if I was only a page in the notebook of your life, you will always be a favorite chapter in mine.

To my mentors: I appreciate your candor and investment in me. I would not be where I am today without your belief in me and willingness to push me to be better.

To my fellow veterans who served as inspiration—Lt Col (Ret) Dave Grossman, Lewis Greer, Jack Carr, Jocko Willink, Admiral (Ret.) Bill McRaven, Marcus Luttrell, Adam Driver, Tom Selleck, Brad Taylor, David Goggins, Tulsi Gabbard, Rob Riggle, Dakota Meyer, Stephen Coonts, Ryan Pote, Peter Blaber, and countless others: Thank you for paving the way for someone like me and inspiring innumerable others. I am honored to be associated with men and women of your caliber.

ABOUT THE AUTHOR

Kevin Kidder is a distinguished leader with twenty years of service in the United States Army, the majority of which were spent in leadership roles. Transitioning from military service, he discovered firsthand the struggles of identity, purpose, and connection that many veterans face once the uniform comes off.

Out of that journey came *The Invisible Veteran*, his first book, written to help service members and their families reclaim purpose and build lives of meaning beyond the military. As evidenced by this project, Kevin is passionate about leadership, personal growth, and building communities where veterans and spouses are seen, valued, and equipped for the next chapter of life.

He currently lives in Michigan and is enrolled in Brian Cain's Mental Performance Mastery certification course. Kevin is also the founder of Emerging Mindset Enterprise (EME), a leadership and personal development company dedicated to helping veterans and their families reclaim purpose, identity, and connection beyond the uniform. Through EME, Kevin continues his lifelong mission of service—not on the battlefield but in the arena of personal growth and transformation.